Inscriptions of the Roman Empire, AD 14-117

Second Edition

LACTOR Sourcebooks in Ancient History

For more than half a century, *LACTOR Sourcebooks in Ancient History* have been providing for the needs of students at schools and universities who are studying ancient history in English translation. Each volume focuses on a particular period or topic and offers a generous and judicious selection of primary texts in new translations. The texts selected include not only extracts from important literary sources but also numerous inscriptions, coin legends and extracts from legal and other texts, which are not otherwise easy for students to access. Many volumes include annotation as well as a glossary, maps and other relevant illustrations, and sometimes a short Introduction. The volumes are written and reviewed by experienced teachers of ancient history at both schools and universities. The series is now being published in print and digital form by Cambridge University Press, with plans for both new editions and completely new volumes.

Inscriptions of the Roman Empire, AD 14-117

Second Edition

____

Edited by
B. H. WARMINGTON
University of Bristol

and

S. J. MILLER
Eton College

CAMBRIDGE
UNIVERSITY PRESS

CAMBRIDGE
UNIVERSITY PRESS

Shaftesbury Road, Cambridge CB2 8EA, United Kingdom

One Liberty Plaza, 20th Floor, New York, NY 10006, USA

477 Williamstown Road, Port Melbourne, VIC 3207, Australia

314–321, 3rd Floor, Plot 3, Splendor Forum, Jasola District Centre, New Delhi – 110025, India

103 Penang Road, #05–06/07, Visioncrest Commercial, Singapore 238467

Cambridge University Press is part of Cambridge University Press & Assessment, a department of the University of Cambridge.

We share the University's mission to contribute to society through the pursuit of education, learning and research at the highest international levels of excellence.

www.cambridge.org
Information on this title: www.cambridge.org/9781009383288
DOI: 10.1017/9781009383301

First published 2023

A catalogue record for this publication is available from the British Library.

A Cataloging-in-Publication data record for this book is available from the Library of Congress.

ISBN978-1-009-38328-8 Paperback

TABLE OF CONTENTS

INTRODUCTION AND ACKNOWLEDGEMENTS

This selection arose out of the need for those studying the JACT "A" level syllabus for the period 14–117 to have epigraphic and numismatic evidence readily available to them in translation; it is hoped, however, that other students and teachers may find the collection of interest.

One hundred documents have been selected and (largely) annotated by Mr. B. H. Warmington of Bristol University; I am deeply indebted to him for this work and for his generous assistance in checking and correcting.

I am also most grateful to Mr. M. Crawford of Christ's College, Cambridge for his work on the coins, and to the following for their translations: H. D. Amos (Wellington College), J. A. Bolton (The Department of Education, Queen's University, Belfast), Miss P. M. Davies (Queen's College, Harley Street), M. A. Edwards (Monkton Combe), R. M. Moody (Epsom College), W. H. Moseley (Eton College), M. A. Murphy (Digby Stuart College of Education), J. Murrell (St. Michael's School, Stevenage), M. A. Nash (Epsom College); and to Dr. J. C. Mann of Durham University for many valuable suggestions and emendations. For the errors and inconsistencies which remain I alone am responsible and I beg the reader's pardon.

Eton College, 1971   S. J. MILLER

I should like to thank Malcolm Young for this elegant resetting of LACTOR 8.

The work of resetting and updating the LACTOR series will continue.

January 1996   JOHN ROBERTS
                                                                  General Editor

NOTES

The arrangement of the entries follows a similar pattern to that of LACTOR 4, *Inscriptions of Roman Britain*. Each entry consists of

(1) number, title and date of dedication or issue (where known);

(2) reference to the original document, first in the standard collections for the history of this period (Ehrenberg and Jones, McCrum and Woodhead, and the two Smallwood volumes), then in the major epigraphic and numismatic collections (*ILS, IG, IGRR, BMC*, etc.; also *CIL* in the Concordances);

(3) site, type of material, when and where found, and where at present located (where known);

(4) translation;

(5) notes, partly from the translators, Dr. J. C. Mann, and S. J. Miller, but largely from B. H. Warmington.

Items which have also been translated in Lewis and Reinhold or in A. H. M. Jones' *History of Rome* have been noted in the Concordances.

The collection is arranged in chronological order of emperors, and approximately twenty-five items have been chosen from each of the four standard collections.

All dates are AD unless otherwise stated.

ABBREVIATIONS
A. EPIGRAPHIC, NUMISMATIC AND GENERAL

AVG. AVGVST. }	Augustus *or* Augusta
CAES.	Caesar
cf.	compare
ch.	chapter
CLAVD.	Claudius
COS.	consul
coss.suff.	suffect (substitute) consuls
DAC.	Dacicus (Conqueror of Dacia)
DESIGN.	*designatus* (designated)
F.	*filius* (son)
ff.	and the following pages
GERM.	Germanicus (Conqueror of Germany)
IMP.	Emperor, *or* "Hailed as *Imperator*" (plus numeral for the number of times)
nr.	near
P.M.	pontifex maximus
P.P.	*pater patriae* (Father of his Country)
P.R.	*populus Romanus* (the Roman People)
S.C.	*senatus consulto* (by decree of the Senate)
sc.	understand something omitted
S.P.Q.R.	*Senatus PopulusQue Romanus* (the Senate and People of Rome)
TI.	Tiberius
TR.P. TR.POT. }	*tribunicia potestate* (with tribunician power)
[ ]	restored by an editor
( )	explanation by editor, *or* addition by translator

B. BOOKS AND PERIODICALS

AHMJ	A. H. M. Jones, *A History of Rome through the Fifth Century: Volume II: The Empire.*
AJP	*American Journal of Philology.*
Arch. Anz.	*Archäologischer Anzeiger.* Beiblatt zum *Jarhbuch des Deutschen Archäologischen Instituts.*
BMC, *Imp.* 1	H. Mattingly, *Coins of the Roman Empire in the British Museum,* Vol. I.
BMC, *Imp.* 3	H. Mattingly, *Coins of the Roman Empire in the British Museum,* Vol. III.
CRAI	*Comptes rendus de l'Académie des Inscriptions et Belles-Lettres.*
CIL	*Corpus Inscriptionum Latinarum.*
EJ	V. Ehrenberg and A. H. M. Jones, *Documents illustrating the Reigns of Augustus and Tiberius.*
FIRA	*Fontes Iuris Romani Anteiustiniani.*
Gordon	A. E. Gordon, *Album of dated Latin Inscriptions,* I.
IG	*Inscriptiones Graecae.*
IGRR	*Inscriptiones Graecae ad Res Romanas pertinentes.*
ILA	S. Gsell, *Inscriptions latines de l'Algérie.*
ILGN	E. Espérandieu, *Inscriptions latines de Gaule (Narbonnaise).*
ILS	H. Dessau, *Inscriptiones Latinae Selectae.*
IRT	J. M. Reynolds and J. B. Ward Perkins, *The Inscriptions of Roman Tripolitania.*
JRS	*Journal of Roman Studies*
LACTOR 4	*Inscriptions of Roman Britain*
LACTOR 11	*Literary Sources for Roman Britain*
LACTOR 15	*Dio: the Julio-Claudians*
LR	N. Lewis and M. Reinhold, *Roman Civilization, Sourcebook II: The Empire.*
MW	M. McCrum and A. G. Woodhead, *Select Documents of the Principates of the Flavian Emperors,* AD 68–96.
NdS	*Notizie degli Scavi di Antichità.*
OGIS	W. Dittenberger, *Orientis Graeci Inscriptiones Selectae.*
P. Lond.	*Greek Papyri in the British Museum.*
RIB	R. G. Collingwood and R. P. Wright, *The Roman Inscriptions of Britain.*
SEG	*Supplementum Epigraphicum Graecum.*
Sel. Pap.	C. C. Edgar and A. S. Hunt, *Select Papyri.*
SG	E. M. Smallwood, *Documents illustrating the Principates of Gaius, Claudius and Nero.*
SIG³	W. Dittenberger, *Sylloge Inscriptionum Graecarum,* 3rd. edition.
SN	E. M. Smallwood, *Documents illustrating the Principates of Nerva, Trajan and Hadrian.*
YCS	*Yale Classical Studies.*

I. FROM TIBERIUS TO NERO

(a) TIBERIUS

1   The Death of Gaius Caesar makes Tiberius the heir-apparent.   AD 4

EJ 69 = *ILS* 140. *Marble slab found at Pisa*, 1606.

In the forum at Pisa in the Augusteum(?)[1] in the presence of the following councillors *(twelve names)* it was mentioned that the decisions set out below were taken when our colony had no magistrates because of the disputes over elections.

News arrived on 2 April that Gaius Caesar, son of Augustus (father of his country, *pontifex maximus*, guardian of the Roman empire and protector of the whole world), grandson of deified Julius, after the successful completion of his consulship campaigning beyond the furthermost territories of the Roman people, and doing noble service to the state in thoroughly conquering or winning over extremely large and warlike tribes, sustained wounds in the public service, and thanks to that misfortune was snatched by cruel fates from the Roman people, already marked out to be a *princeps* of the highest worth, most like his father in excellence, and the sole protector of our colony. The news renewed and multiplied for everybody, both individually and as a group, the grief which was still felt as a result of the death of Lucius Caesar, Gaius' brother, consul elect, augur, our patron, leader of the youth.

Accordingly the decurions and all the other colonists, in the absence of duovirs, prefects and judicial officers in the colony at this sad time, agreed unanimously, in view of the magnitude of the enormous and utterly unexpected disaster, that from the day when his death was announced until the day when his bones should be brought home and buried and the proper rites completed for his departed spirit, all should wear mourning, all the temples of the immortal gods, the public baths and shops should be closed, there should be no banquets, the wives in our colony should mourn publicly, that the day of his death, 21 February, should be remembered in mourning like the Allia, to be noted as nefarious at the present time by unanimous will and approval, and precautions should be taken to prevent any public sacrifice, thanksgivings, marriages or public feasts being held, planned or advertised for or on that day, 21 February. No theatrical shows or circuses should take place on that day. Every year on that day there should be solemn public sacrifices to his departed spirit made by the magistrates or the judicial officers at Pisa in the same place and manner as for Lucius Caesar.[2] An arch should be set up in the most popular place in our colony decorated with the spoils of tribes whom he conquered or won over; on it should be a statue of him standing in triumphal dress, and around it

---

[1] The conjectured opening is based on EJ 68 (= *ILS* 139).
[2] For details see EJ 68.

should be two gilded statues of Gaius and Lucius Caesar on horseback. As soon as we could elect and have according to law duovirs of the colony, those first elected as duovirs should bring before the decurions the decision of the decurions and the whole colony, so that it could be legally enacted by the exercise of their public authority and put on the public record with their approval. Meanwhile Titus Statulenus Juncus, *flamen* of Augustus, *pontifex minor* of the public sacrifices of the Roman people, should be asked to go with envoys to excuse the present deficiency of the colony and in delivering a written report to inform the emperor Caesar Augustus, father of his country, *pontifex maximus*, holder of tribunician power twenty-six times, of this public service and wish of the whole colony. Titus Statulenus Juncus, leader of our colony, *flamen* of Augustus, *pontifex minor* of the public sacrifices of the Roman people, has done this after delivering the report as recorded above to the emperor Caesar Augustus, *pontifex maximus*, holder of tribunician power twenty-six times, father of his country.

The decurions decreed that all that was done, enacted, and decided on 2 April in the consulship of Sextus Aelius Cato and Gaius Sentius Saturninus by unanimous consent of all classes should be done, carried out, conducted and observed by Lucius Titius, son of Aulus, and Titus Allius Rufus, son of Titus, duovirs, and should be enacted, established, marked and observed for ever by whomsoever should be duovirs, prefects or other magistrates in our colony hereafter. Lucius Titius, son of Aulus, and Titus Allius Rufus, son of Titus, duovirs, should attend to the entry in the public records by the public scribe in the presence of the proquaestors of all the above by our decree at the first opportunity. Approved.

The death of Gaius Caesar from wounds received on active service in Armenia, following so soon upon that of the only other grandson of Augustus, Lucius, at Marseilles (2), meant that Augustus had no alternative but to adopt Tiberius as his heir to the principate. The apparently extravagant terms of the decree perhaps reflected unease that the problem of succession to Augustus was again open. Augustus himself never concealed his grief (*Res Gestae* 14; Suetonius, *Tiberius* 23).

2   Sestertius of Tiberius: Julia Augusta.   AD 22–23

EJ 87 = *BMC, Imp.* 1, p.130, nos. 76ff. *Mint of Rome.*

> *Obverse:* S.C. TI. CAESAR DIVI AVG. F. AVGVST. P.M. TR. POT. XXIII
>
> *Reverse:* Coach *(carpentum)* with mules. S.P.Q.R. IVLIAE AVGVST.

Tiberius' mother Livia became Julia Augusta after the death of Augustus. Cf. nos. 3, 4, 7(b), 21 and 37.

3   Decree on Imperial cult and letter of Tiberius.   [? AD 14–15]

EJ 102 = *SEG* 11.922–3 *Gytheum (Laconia).*

(a)   ... he shall set ... on the first [pedestal the statue] of deified Augustus Caesar, his father; on the second, to the right, that of Julia Augusta, and on the third, [to the left,] that of the emperor Tiberius Caesar, son of Augustus, the city providing him with the statues. He shall put a table in the middle of the theatre and set a censer on it, and the councillors and all the magistrates shall offer sacrifice for the safety of our rulers before the performers enter. The performance on the first day shall honour the deified Augustus, our saviour and deliverer, son of deified Julius Caesar, on the second the emperor Tiberius Caesar Augustus, father of his country, on the third Julia Augusta, the Good Fortune of our province and city, on the fourth the Victory of Germanicus Caesar, on the fifth the Venus of Drusus Caesar, on the sixth Titus Quinctius Flamininus ...[1]

When the procession reaches the temple of Caesar, the superintendents shall sacrifice a bull for the safety of our rulers and gods and for the perpetuity of their rule ...[1]

(b) Tiberius Caesar Augustus, son of Augustus, *pontifex maximus*, holding the tribunician power for the [sixteenth] year, to the superintendents and city of Gytheum, greeting. Decimus Turranius Nicanor, the envoy sent by you to me and my mother, gave me your letter to which were appended the measures passed by you in veneration of my father and in our honour. I commend you for this and consider that it is fitting for all men in general and for your city in particular to reserve special honours befitting the gods in keeping with the greatness of the services of my father to the whole world; but I myself am satisfied with more moderate honours suitable for men. My mother, however, will reply to you when she hears your decision about honours for her.

Tiberius apparently had a genuine aversion to receiving divine honours even from the provinces. Claudius expressed a similar feeling: see no. 27. Cf. next item and no. 7(b).

The importance of Julia Augusta or Livia, widow of Augustus and mother of Tiberius, is notable; she is referred to in the phrase "safety of our rulers". Cf. nos. 2, 4, 7(b), 21 and 37.

4   Decree on emperor-worship   AD 18

EJ 101 = *ILS* 154. *Bracciano* (Forum Clodii, Etruria); *now in Florence.*

In the year of the third consulship of Tiberius Caesar and the second consulship of Germanicus Caesar, when Gnaeus Acceius Rufus Lutatius, son of Gnaeus, of the tribe *Arnensis* and Titus Petillius, son of Publius, of the tribe *Quirina*, were duovirs, it was decreed as follows:

that there be this shrine and these statues and a sacrificial victim for the feast of dedication;

that on 23 and 24 September, two sacrificial animals are to be offered up for the birthday of Augustus (24 September) as have been offered up from all time at the altar which has been dedicated to the Augustan divinity;

---

[1] A good deal of further detail (some 70% of the decree) is omitted.

that in the same way, on the birthday of Tiberius Caesar, the decurions who are to enter office, and the people, should partake of a banquet, (Quintus Cascellius Labeo has promised to meet the expense for all time, so that our gratitude for his generosity must be noted) and that every year, on that birthday, a young bull must be sacrificed;

that on the birthdays of Augustus and Tiberius Caesar, before the decurions go to have their meal, the spirits of those emperors should be invited with incense and wine to partake of a feast at the altar of the Augustan divinity.

At our expense we have built an altar to the Augustan divinity; at our own expense we have celebrated games for five days beginning on 15 August; at our own expense we have given honey-wine and pastries on the birthday of the Empress to the women of the village at the temple of the Good Goddess; similarly at our own expense on the occasion of the dedication of the statues of the Caesars and of the Empress, we have given honey-wine and pastries to the decurions and to the people, and we have given solemn assurances that we will continue to do so for all time on the anniversary of the dedication. In order to make that day more popular as years go by, we will set aside 10 March, the day upon which Tiberius Caesar was so happily made *pontifex maximus*.

This inscription illustrates the nature of imperial worship in Italy shortly after the death of Augustus. The altar is dedicated *numini Augusto*, the Augustan divinity, and "royal" birthdays are celebrated in quasi-religious manner. Augustus' wife Livia became Julia Augusta after his death, cf. nos. 2, 3, 7(b), 21 and 37. Distinctions must be made with the eastern part of the empire (see next item); there was no cult in Italy and the west of the Emperor as a person, cf. no. 3.

5   Tiberius the god.   16 November AD 29

EJ 134 = *OGIS* 583. *Stone pedestal found in Lapethus, Cyprus in 1861.*

To the god Tiberius Caesar Augustus, son of deified Augustus, emperor, *pontifex maximus*, holder of tribunician power for the thirty-first time – when Lucius Axius Naso was proconsul, Marcus Etrilius Lupercus legate and Gaius Flavius Figulus quaestor – Adrastus, son of Adrastus, friend of Caesar, the hereditary priest of the temple and statue of Tiberius Caesar Augustus which was set up by him at his own expense in the gymnasium; patriot and model of all virtue, gymnasiarch freely and at his own expense; priest of the gods in the gymnasium, set up the temple and the statue to his god at his own personal expense. Dionysius, son of Dionysius also called Apollodotus, friend of Caesar, was ephebarch. Adrastus, son of Adrastus, friend of Caesar dedicated them together with his son Adrastus, friend of Caesar, who was himself gymnasiarch of the boys, freely and at his own expense, on the sixteenth anniversary of Tiberius, the 24th. day of the month Apogonicus.

See Suetonius, *Tiberius* 26 on Tiberius' careful control of worship of himself which, however, he could not prevent in eastern provinces. See also nos. 3, 4, 7(b).

6 Didrachm of Caligula. AD 37–38?

EJ 182 = *BMC, Imp.* 1, p.62, no.104. *Mint of Caesarea.*

> *Obverse:* Head of Germanicus; around, GERMANICVS CAESAR TI. AVG. F. COS.II.

> *Reverse:* Germanicus placing tiara on head of Artaxias; beside Germanicus, GERMANICVS; beside Artaxias, ARTAXIAS.

Tiberius refused to recognise Vonones, who had been driven from the throne of Parthia, as king of Armenia. He failed to maintain himself, and the Armenians pressed for the installation of Zeno, son of Polemo king of Pontus. In 18 Germanicus crowned him at Artaxata, from which he derived his new name of Artaxias (Tacitus, *Annals* 2.56). The coin appears to have been issued in Germanicus' honour by his son Caligula.

7 Two edicts of Germanicus. AD 19

EJ 320 = *Sel. Pap.* 2, no.211. *Papyrus.*

(a) [Germanicus Caesar, son of Augustus, grandson of deified Augustus, proconsul, says: "Hearing that in regard to my visit, requisitions of boats] and animals are being made, and that quarters for lodgings are being forcibly seized and private citizens intimidated, I have thought it necessary to make it plain that I do not wish any boat or any baggage animal to be seized by anyone, or any quarters to be occupied, except on the command of Baebius, my friend and secretary. For if it is necessary, Baebius himself will allot the quarters fairly and justly. And for boats and animals that are requisitioned I give orders that due payment is to be made according to my schedule. Those who oppose *(this)*, I wish to be brought before my secretary who will himself prevent private persons from being wronged or will report the case to me. I forbid baggage animals which are travelling through the city to be forcibly taken off by those who happen to meet them. For this is simply an act of confessed robbery."

(b) Germanicus Caesar, son of Augustus, grandson of deified Augustus, proconsul, says: "Your goodwill, which you display whenever you see me, I welcome, but your acclamations, which are odious to me and which are suited to the gods, I wholly reject. For they are suitable only for the one who is indeed the saviour and the benefactor of the whole human race, my father, and to his mother, my grandmother. My position is [?consequent upon] their divinity, so that, if you disobey me, you will compel me to appear before you seldom."

See Tacitus, *Annals* 2.59–61 for Germanicus' famous visit to Egypt in 19, "to visit the antiquities" *(cognoscendae antiquitatis)*; Tacitus tried to argue that this was in breach of Augustus' prohibition of senators' visiting Egypt without permission; see also F. B. Marsh, *Tiberius* 93.

(a) Illustrates the ineradicable abuses of power (especially current in Egypt) even under the improved administration of the Empire; cf. no. 50.

(b) On the standard rejection of divine honours cf. no. 27 by Claudius, also referring to the Alexandrians. On Tiberius' policy cf. no. 3; see also nos. 4 and 5.

8   *Rogation* in honour of Germanicus.   AD 19–20

EJ 94a = *NdS* (1947) p.49ff; *AJP* (1954) p.225 *(revised text)*. Heba *(Etruria)*.

... and that on the Palatine in the colonnade near the temple of Apollo, in which meetings of the senate are customarily held, among the busts of heroes busts shall be set up of Germanicus Caesar of famous ability and of Drusus Germanicus, his father, brother of Tiberius Caesar Augustus, who was also a man of prolific ability, above the capitals of the columns which protect the statue of Apollo.

The Salii shall insert the name of Germanicus Caesar in their hymns as a tribute to his memory, a tribute also granted to Gaius and Lucius Caesar, brothers of Tiberius Caesar Augustus.

To the ten centuries which customarily vote to pre-elect the consuls and praetors shall be added five centuries; since the first ten are called Gaius and Lucius Caesar's, the five following shall be called Germanicus Caesar's. In all those centuries the senators and knights of all the decuries established already or in the future for public trials shall vote.

(There follow lengthy amendments of the existing law on electoral procedure necessitated by the five new centuries).

When at the games in honour of Augustus the seats of his priests are put in the theatres, curule chairs for Germanicus Caesar shall be put among them and crowns of oak leaves in honour of that priesthood. These chairs shall be brought from the temple of deified Augustus when it is finished; meanwhile they shall be put back in the temple of Mars the Avenger and brought from there. Whoever conducts the aforementioned games shall have charge of taking the chairs from the aforementioned temple, placing them in the theatres and putting them back in that temple at the right time.

On the day when the bones of Germanicus Caesar are to be brought to the tomb the temples of the gods shall be closed. Those enrolled in the equestrian class with a private horse, who wish to perform their duty and are not prevented by illness or a death in the family, shall come to the *Campus Martius* wearing their striped tunic, and those with a public horse shall come wearing their striped robe.

In honour of Germanicus Caesar the temples of the immortal gods which are or shall be in Rome or within one mile of the city shall be closed every year on the day of his death. Those who have or will have contracts for the care of those temples shall see to this. On that day in his honour the annual masters of the priests of Augustus shall see to it that sacrifices to the dead are made at his tomb to the *di manes* of Germanicus Caesar. If one or more of the masters will be unable to be present at that sacrifice, those due to fill that office in the following year will carry out that duty in place of those unable to perform it.

On the importance of this text, the so-called *Tabula Hebana*, see A. H. M. Jones, *Studies in Roman Government and Law* 29–50. The five centuries of Germanicus, added to the ten centuries of Gaius and Lucius Caesar, all consisting of senators and equites, gave the lead to the voting in the *comitia centuriata* for the magistrates. Since in 14 Tiberius apparently arranged that the Senate should settle among themselves the candidates, and that their number should not exceed the number of places to be filled, the election in the Assembly became a mere formality.

9   Tiberius and Piso.   7 BC

EJ 39 = *ILS* 95. *A marble base found in Rome in the Campus Martius*, 1547.

> Tiberius Claudius Nero, son of Tiberius, *pontifex*, consul for the second time, twice hailed as *Imperator*, celebrated games of thanksgiving to Jupiter Best and Greatest, in accordance with a resolution of the senate in honour of the return of Augustus Caesar, *pontifex maximus*, son of deified Julius Caesar ...
>
> *Erased:* with his colleague in the consulship Gnaeus Calpurnius Piso.

Piso, a proud and forceful personality, was a friend of Augustus and Tiberius. In 17 he was appointed *legatus* of Syria and given confidential instructions on how to handle Germanicus' visit to the East. The two fell out and after Germanicus' death Piso was accused of poisoning him; seeing that his judges were bent on returning a verdict of "Guilty", he committed suicide. The erasure of his name (Tacitus, *Annals* 2.43 ff, 3. 10 ff.) from public monuments was ordered by the Senate.

10   Sestertius of Tiberius: Tiberius helps Asian cities.   AD 22–23

EJ 49 = *BMC, Imp.* 1, p.129, nos. 70 ff. *Mint of Rome.*

> *Obverse:* In centre, S(ENATVS) C(ONSVLTO); around, TI. CAESAR DIVI AVG. F. AVGVST. P.M. TR. POT. XXIIII.
>
> *Reverse:* Tiberius seated on curule chair; around, CIVITATIBVS ASIAE RESTITVTIS = *(in record of)* the restoration of the cities of Asia.

The reverse legend alludes to the financial help given by Tiberius to the cities devastated by earthquake in 17 (Tacitus, *Annals* 2.47; Pliny, *Natural History* 2.200) and 23 (Tacitus, *Annals* 4.13). In 17 Sardis received five years' remission of taxes and ten million sesterces. Cf. EJ 50 = *ILS* 156, in which help to Ephesus, devastated in 29, is also recorded.

11   Drusus, heir-apparent of Tiberius.   AD 23

EJ 90 = *NdS* (1924) p.514. *Near Caudium.*

> To Drusus Caesar, son of Tiberius Augustus, grandson of deified Augustus, great-grandson of deified Julius, twice consul, holder of tribunician power for the second time.

Drusus had been excluded from the succession when Tiberius was forced to adopt Germanicus, so that direct descendants of Augustus by Germanicus' wife Agrippina would ultimately rule. On Germanicus' death in 19, Drusus became heir-apparent, as Germanicus' children were too young. He received a second consulship in 21 and tribunician power for the second time in 23. His death in 23 was attributed to Sejanus and Drusus' wife Livilla. See F. B. Marsh, *Tiberius, passim*.

12   The father of Sejanus.

EJ 220 = *ILS* 8996. *Marble tablet found in Bolsena* (Volsinii?), *now in the Archaeological Museum in Florence.*

> [Lucius Seius Strabo] prefect of Egypt and Terentia, his mother, daughter of Aulus, and Cosconia Galitta his wife, daughter of Lentulus Maluginensis, having bought the buildings and razed them to the ground, gave the baths with all their equipment to the people of Volsinii for public use.

See Tacitus, *Annals* 4.1. Seius Strabo married into a noble family (the Cornelii Lentuli). His son was probably adopted by Aelius Gallus, hence his full name Lucius Aelius Seianus. Strabo was praetorian prefect in 14 and was joined in the office by his son; soon after, he became prefect of Egypt.

13   Consulship of Sejanus.

EJ 53 = *ILS* 6044. *Found in Rome, now in Naples.*

> ... since now ... sixty years of age ... and sinister assembly sponsored by the traitorous Sejanus and held on the Aventine hill when he was made consul, I now most earnestly entreat you to permit me to present myself as a suppliant, though now reduced to a helpless state where my stick is my constant companion, my good fellow-tribesmen, asking you to remember that I have always appeared before you as a never-failing and reliable member of our tribe, that I have never neglected my duty, nor in any respect ...

On Sejanus, see also nos. 12 and 14–16. Suetonius, *Tiberius* 65, refers to the nomination of Sejanus as consul by Tiberius, with himself as colleague, for 31. The electoral formalities naturally followed.

14   A close friend of Tiberius.

EJ 217 = *ILGN* 633. *Marble fragment found in Castel Roussillon* (Ruscino, Narbonensis) *in 1911.*

> To Publius Memmius Regulus, son of Publius, quaestor of Tiberius Caesar, praetor, consul, member of the board of seven for supervising sacrificial banquets, priest of Augustus, member of the Arval Brothers, imperial legate, patron.

Regulus, close friend of Tiberius, was consul at the end of 31 and probably Tiberius' chief confidant in the destruction of Sejanus, cf. nos. 13 and 15–16. He was just possibly a native of Ruscino. His post as "emperor's quaestor" shows that he was marked out early for promotion. He was governor of Moesia, Macedonia and Achaea (35–44), and remained influential under Claudius and Nero, dying in 61. Tacitus' statement that Nero regarded him as a possible emperor if he himself died is generally regarded as unhistorical (*Annals* 14.47). For patrons see no. 19 *note*.

15 Thanksgiving for the fall of Sejanus. AD 32

EJ 51 = *ILS* 157. *Interamna (Umbria).*

> Faustus Titius Liberalis, when for the second time a member of the college of priests of Augustus, at his own expense erected this
>
> to the everlasting Augustan peace and the political freedom of the Roman people,
>
> to the genius which protects the town of Interamna, in the seven hundred and fourth year after its foundation, as mark of honour to the consuls Gnaeus Domitius Ahenobarbus and Lucius Arruntius Camillus Scribonianus,
>
> to the statesmanship of Tiberius Caesar, son of Augustus, in honour of the imperishable name of Rome upon the occasion of the extermination of a deadly foe of the Roman people.

Scribonianus, legate of Dalmatia, led a revolt in 42; deserted by his troops, he committed suicide. Since he was declared a public enemy, the words "and Lucius Arruntius Camillus Scribonianus" were erased from this inscription in 42.

The "deadly foe" was Sejanus, declared *hostis publicus* by the senate in 31 and executed. For his conspiracy, see R. Syme, *Tacitus*, 404–6.

16 A compliment to Tiberius. AD 32–33

EJ 85 = *ILS* 159. *Rignano, near the Via Flaminia in the district of Capena.*

> Aulus Fabius Fortunatus, attendant on the consuls and praetors, first priest of Augustus, in fulfilment of his vow, has set this up to Tiberius Caesar Augustus, son of deified Augustus, *pontifex maximus,* consul five times, holder of the tribunician power for the thirty-third time, our most worthy *princeps* and most just and honourable protector of our country, for his safety and well-being.

Perhaps a reference to the general unease caused by the Sejanus affair.

17 An important senator under Tiberius. AD 35–36

EJ 218a = *IRT* 330. *One pair of inscriptions on a limestone arch, Lepcis Magna.*

> To Tiberius Caesar Augustus, son of deified Augustus, grandson of deified Julius, *pontifex maximus,* consul five times, eight times hailed as *Imperator,* in the thirty-seventh year of his tribunician power, Gaius Rubellius Blandus, quaestor of deified Augustus, plebeian tribune, praetor, consul, proconsul, *pontifex,* patron *(erected this).* From the revenues of the lands which he restored to the people of Lepcis, he arranged the paving of all the roads of the community of Lepcis. Marcus Etrilius Lupercus, propraetorian legate, patron *(of the city),* supervised the auction of this work.

Rubellius Blandus, of a relatively undistinguished family, was early marked out for promotion as his office of quaestor of Augustus indicates. Consul in 18, he married Julia, daughter of Tiberius' son Drusus in 33. The work at Lepcis Magna was perhaps the aftermath of the revolt of Tacfarinas (cf. no. 20), and he was made patron of the city, like many other proconsuls (see no. 19 *note*).

On the death in 62 of his son Rubellius Plautus, because of his relationship with the imperial house, see Tacitus, *Annals* 14.22 and 57–9.

18   Gaius "Caligula", heir-apparent?   AD 33–37

EJ 97 = *ILS* 189. *Vienne* (Vienna, Narbonensis).

> To Gaius Caesar Germanicus, son of Germanicus, grandson of Tiberius Augustus and great-grandson of deified Augustus, *pontifex* and quaestor.

The youngest son of Germanicus, Gaius only emerges as potential successor to Tiberius after the deaths of his brothers and the fall of Sejanus. Even then Tiberius, in his suspicion, refused to give more than a priesthood and the quaestorship (33). However, his prospects appear to have been recognised by some.

19   A patron-client agreement.   AD 28?

EJ 354 = *ILS* 6099. Tessera patronatus, *near Brixia.*

> On 5 December in the consulship of Lucius Silanus, *flamen* of Mars, and Gaius Vellaeus Tutor, the senate and people of Siagu formed a friendship with Gaius Silius Aviola, son of Gaius, of the tribe *Fabia*, military tribune of the third legion *Augusta*, "commander of the engineers"[1] and chose him and his descendants as patron of themselves and their descendants. Gaius Silius Aviola, son of Gaius, of the tribe of *Fabia*, received them and their descendants under his protection as clients. Transacted by Celer, son of Imilcho Gulalsa, *sufet*.

This was the standard form of recording an agreement between client and patron when the client was a community. Cf. nos. 1, 14, 17, 19, 25, 37, 59, 81, and 87 for other patrons of communities. In this case the patron was of fairly modest rank, who had presumably come to the notice of Siagu (in Tunisia) during service with the third legion *Augusta* in Africa, or perhaps as "commander of the engineers" of the proconsul of Africa, for three other patronage agreements are known which Aviola made with African communities, all in northern Tunisia. Cf. no. 32 for another *sufet*, chief magistrate of a Punic town.

20   King Ptolemy of Mauretania.   AD 29–30

EJ 163 = *Mélanges Gautier* (1937), 332. *Caesarea, Mauretania.*

> For the welfare of king Ptolemy, son of king Juba, in the tenth year of his reign, I, Antistia Galla, willingly and deservedly paid this vow to Saturn, having received the sacrificial offering from Julia Vitalis, daughter of Respectus, of Rusguniae.

Ptolemy, son of Juba II of Mauretania and Cleopatra Selene (daughter of Cleopatra), succeeded to the throne on the death of his father (23–24). He assisted in campaigns against Tacfarinas (*c.* 17–24) which may have facilitated his recog-

---

[1] See no. 23 *note.*

nition on his father's death (cf. Tacitus, *Annals* 4.26). He was summoned to Rome by the emperor Gaius and murdered (40) (Suetonius, *Gaius* 35.1), his kingdom being turned into two provinces by Claudius after the suppression of a revolt. Rusguniae was a colony of Augustus on the Algerian coast. For Saturn cf. no. 25.

21   An equestrian career.

EJ 225 = *Arch. Anz.* (1940), 521. *Silver bust of Tiberius, posthumous, Teate Marrucinorum.*

> To Tiberius Caesar Augustus, son of deified Augustus, *pontifex maximus*, holder of tribunician power thirty-eight times, consul five times, by the will of Marcus Pulfennius, son of Sextus, of the tribe *Arnensis*, centurion of the sixth legion *Ferrata*, Gaius Herennius Capito, son of Titus, of the tribe *Arnensis*, military tribune for three tours of duty, prefect of cavalry, prefect of veterans, procurator of Julia Augusta, procurator of Tiberius Caesar Augustus, procurator of Gaius Caesar Augustus Germanicus, with ten pounds of silver *(dedicated this)*.

Capito's procuratorship was in the small principality bequeathed by Salome, sister of Herod the Great, to Livia (Julia Augusta) for whom cf. nos. 2–4, 7(b), and 37. He remained in control when the property passed to Tiberius in 29 and to Caligula in 37.

22   An equestrian career.

EJ 243 = *ILS* 1349. *Bronze tablet, found at Zuglio* (Iulium Carnicum) *in 1811, now in the museum at Cividale.*

> To Gaius Baebius Atticus, son of Publius, of the tribe *Claudia*, judicial duovir, senior centurion of the fifth legion *Macedonica*, prefect of the communities of Moesia and Treballia, prefect of the communities in the Maritime Alps, military tribune of the eighth praetorian cohort, senior centurion for a second time, procurator of Tiberius Claudius Caesar Augustus Germanicus in Noricum, the community of the Saevates and Laeanci *(set this up)*.

The title of *procurator* for equestrian governors of small provinces became general under Claudius; previously *praefectus* was usual. Baebius was probably a native of the community which honoured him.

23   A distinguished equestrian career.

EJ 245 = *ILS* 2690. *Inscription on stone, found near Venafrum, now erased.*

> Lusia Paullina, daughter of Marcus, wife of Sextus Vettulenus Cerealis, *(erected this)* for herself and her father Marcus Vergilius Gallus Lusius, son of Marcus,[1] of the tribe *Teretina*, senior centurion of the eleventh legion, prefect of the cohort of Ubian infantry and cavalry, awarded two silver spearshafts and golden crowns by deified Augustus and Tiberius Caesar Augustus, "commander of the engineers" three times, military

---

[1] Lusia Paullina's father was originally a Lusius, son of Aulus (like his brother) but was later adopted by a Marcus Vergilius, and thus appears as "son of Marcus".

tribune of the first praetorian cohort, imperial financial administrator in Egypt, duovir twice, *pontifex*; and for his brother Aulus Lusius Gallus, son of Aulus, of the tribe *Teretina*, military tribune of the twenty-second legion *Cyrenaica*,[1] prefect of cavalry.

A typical distinguished military career in the equestrian class during the early empire. The post of *praefectus fabrum* had now no connexion with engineers, and had become a post on the staff of a consul, praetor or proconsul. The career ends with the administration of the emperor's finances in Egypt (*idiologus*).

24   A freedman of Augustus   AD 26

EJ 333 = *ILS* 6579. *Marble tablet found at Veii in* 1691; *now in the Capitoline Museum, Rome.*

When the town council of Augustan Veii met in Rome at the temple of Venus Genetrix, they decided unanimously that, until the decree should be put in writing, in the meantime, Gaius Julius Gelos, freedman of Augustus, who not only helped the town of Veii at all times with his advice and influence, but also wanted to make it famous with his resources and through his son, be allowed to be decreed the most fitting honour: that he be ranked among the priests of Augustus just as if he enjoyed that honour, and be allowed to sit on the special seat of honour among the priests of the cult of Augustus at all the games in our town and to take part in all public feasts among the town councillors. They decided likewise that no tax imposed by the town of Augustan Veii should be exacted from him or his children.

There were present: Gaius Scaevius Curiatius, Lucius Perperna Priscus, duovirs; Marcus Flavius Rufus, quaestor; Titus Vettius Rufus, quaestor; Marcus Tarquitius Saturninus, Lucius Maecilius Scrupus, Lucius Favonius Lucanus, Gnaeus Octavius Sabinus, Titus Sempronius Gracchus, Publius Acuvius, son of Publius of the tribe *Tromentina*, Gaius Veianius Maximus, Titus Tarquitius Rufus, Gaius Julius Merula. Transacted in the consulship of Gaetulicus and Calvisius Sabinus.

Imperial freedmen are traditionally said to have become important under Claudius, but their position from the start was important, as this honorific decree by the city of Veii to a freedman of Augustus shows.

25   Romanisation at Thugga.   AD 36–37

EJ 345 = *Nouvelles archives des missions* (1913), 38. *Dougga* (Thugga), *northern Tunisia.*

To the emperor Tiberius Caesar Augustus, son of deified Augustus, *pontifex maximus*, thirty-eight times holder of tribunician power, five times consul, Lucius Manilius Bucco, son of Lucius, of the tribe *Arnensis*, duovir, made this dedication. Lucius Postumius Chius, son of Gaius, of the tribe *Arnensis*, patron of the district, in his own name and that of his sons Firmus and Rufus, paved the forum and the open space in front of the temple of

---

[1] No legion XXII *Cyrenaica* is known; this is probably an error for XXII *Deiotariana*.

Caesar, and also saw to the erection of an altar of Augustus, a temple of Saturn and an arch, at his own expense.

The majority of the inhabitants of the town at this date were non-Romans, but a number of Roman citizens were resident, forming a *pagus* with their own organisation; some were apparently citizens of the colony of Carthage. Urbanisation and Romanisation began early under the influence of the Roman residents, but note in addition to the imperial cult a temple of Saturn, Roman equivalent of the Punic Baal Hammon; cf. no. 20. For other patrons see no. 19 *note*.

(b) GAIUS CALIGULA

26   An oath of allegiance to Gaius Caligula   11 May AD 37

SG 32 = *ILS* 190. *Stone found at Aritium, Lusitania.*

An oath of the citizens of Aritium to Gaius Ummidius Durmius Quadratus, propraetorian legate of Gaius Caesar Germanicus *Imperator*:

From the deepest conviction, as truly as I shall be the enemy of those whom I learn to be the enemies of Gaius Caesar Germanicus, so I shall not cease to pursue by land and sea with armed force in bitter warfare anyone who endangers or shall endanger him and his safety, until he has paid the penalty to him; I shall consider neither myself nor my children dearer than his safety, and shall regard those who show hostile intentions towards him as my enemies. If I knowingly break my oath now or in the future, then may Jupiter Best and Greatest and deified Augustus and all the rest of the immortal gods deprive me and my children of my country, my safety and all my possessions.

Dated 11 May in the old town of Aritium, in the consulship of Gnaeus Acerronius Proculus and Gaius Petronius Pontius Nigrinus, in the magistracy of Vegetus, son of Tallicus, and – ibius, son of – arionus.

An oath of allegiance sworn on the accession of the emperor Gaius Caligula, showing a time-lag of fifty-two days after the death of Tiberius. Such oaths of allegiance to the emperor were taken by communities throughout the empire.

(c) CLAUDIUS

27   Letter of Claudius to the people of Alexandria   10 November AD 41

SG 370 = *P. Lond.* 1912; *Sel. Pap.* 212. *Papyrus, now in the British Library.*

Lucius Aemilius Rectus states: "Since it was not possible for the whole city on account of its size to be present at the public reading of the most sacred and beneficent letter to the city, I considered it necessary to publish the letter so that each of you individually may read it and wonder at the magnanimity of our god Caesar and return him thanks for his kindness to the whole city." Dated 14th. of New Augustus in the second year of Tiberius Claudius Caesar Augustus Germanicus the emperor.

"Tiberius Claudius Caesar Augustus Germanicus, the emperor, *pontifex maximus*, holder of tribunician power, consul designate, sends greetings to the city of the Alexandrians. Your ambassadors, Tiberius Claudius Barbillus, Apollonis son of Artemidorus, Chaeremon son of Leonidas, Marcus Julius Asclepiades, Gaius Julius Dionysius, Tiberius Claudius Phanias, Pasion son of Potamon, Dionysius son of Sabbio, Tiberius Claudius Archebius, Apollonis son of Ariston, Gaius Julius Apollonius, Hermaiscus son of Apollonius, told me a great deal about your city when they passed on your resolution. They reminded me of your loyalty to me, which I have long treasured, you may be sure. For you, as I have proved on many occasions, are naturally faithful to the Caesars, and have given special support to my house, just as it has to you, as my brother Germanicus Caesar (to omit all other examples) has recently expressed to you in generous terms. And so I was glad to accept the honours which you bestowed on me, although I am not fond of this kind of thing.

"First, I grant that you may treat my birthday as an Augustal day in the way in which you yourselves have indicated. Then I permit you to erect statues of me and my family in any place. For I realise that the establishing of the memorials of your loyalty to my house will be rapidly achieved. With reference to the two golden statues, the one of the Claudian Augustan Peace, which my most honoured Barbillus proposed and persisted in advocating despite my refusal of it for fear of seeming vulgarly arrogant, will be set up at Rome. The other will be carried in your procession as you ask on the days named after me. Moreover you may also take with the statue a chariot adorned as you wish.

"It would perhaps be foolish to allow such honours and yet refuse to introduce a Claudian tribe, or permission to establish sacred groves according to Egyptian custom. And so I allow you to do this in my honour. Set up, too, if you wish, the equestrian statues given by Vitrasius Pollio, my procurator. I grant you permission to set up the four-horse statues which you wish to erect to me at the entries to the country, one at Libyan Taposiris, one near the Pharos in Alexandria, the third at Pelusium.

"The appointment of a high priest to me and the building of temples I decline, since I do not wish to seem arrogant to my own generation, and consider that sacrifices and such honours have been given by men of every age only to the gods.

"With reference to the requests which you pressed me to grant, I give judgement as follows: in the case of all those who came of age up to the beginning of my principate, I confirm and validate the rights of Alexandrian citizenship with all the honours and favours granted to the city. This does not apply to any who have insinuated themselves among you to get the citizenship although they are the children of slaves. It is my wish that all the rest of the favours, too, which you have received from the emperors before me, the kings and the prefects, shall be confirmed, just as deified Augustus confirmed them.

"It is my wish that the guardians of the temples to deified Augustus in Alexandria shall be appointed by lot, just as those in the temple of the same deified Augustus at Canopus are appointed.

"With reference to your request that public offices be held for three years, it seems to me that the decision already reached is very good. For the magistrates will behave more properly towards us in their period of office if they are afraid of their misdemeanours being scrutinised.

"As for the Council, your practice under the former kings I know nothing of; but that you had no council under previous emperors you are perfectly well aware. Since it is a new proposal which is now being mooted for the first time and since it is unclear whether it will benefit the city or my interests, I have written to Aemilius Rectus, asking him to investigate the matter; and he will report to me whether it is necessary to establish this body and, if it is necessary, on the way in which it will be done.

"As for the disturbances and riots against the Jews, which were, indeed, to tell the truth, more like a war, I did not wish to inquire too closely into which party was guilty of them, although your ambassadors and especially Dionysius son of Theon tried very hard to bring accusations. I reserve however the right to show implacable anger against those who start them again. I expressly state that if this presumption and destructive violence against each other does not stop, I shall be forced to show what a merciful emperor is like when he has been aroused to justified anger. I therefore hereby solemnly proclaim that the Alexandrians must behave in a civilised and kindly fashion towards the Jews who have lived in the same city for many years; that they must not interfere in any way with their customary religious rites; that they must allow them to practise these rites as they did under deified Augustus, which right I have confirmed after hearing both sides. Equally I order the Jews not to try to get more than they had before; nor again, as if they lived in two cities, to send two embassies (which never happened before); nor to wreck the games arranged by the gymnasiarchs or the *kosmêtae*. Instead they are to enjoy their own possessions and be glad to have such great wealth in a city which is not their own. They must not introduce or invite in Jews who come by boat from Syria or downstream from Egypt; for, if they do, I shall be forced to entertain greater suspicion of them. If they do not obey these commands, I shall do everything to expel them as those who cause a disease which is common to the whole world.

"If both sides abandon these habits and are willing to live in a civilised and kindly fashion with each other, I too shall hold the city in the highest regard as being linked to my house from the days of my ancestors. Barbillus my friend, I assure you, has always aroused my regard for you, and on this occasion too has been very zealous in the argument on your behalf. The same is true of my friend Tiberius Claudius Archebius, too. Farewell."

For detailed commentary see H. I. Bell, *Jews and Christians in Egypt* (1924), 1–37. See also A. Momigliano, *Claudius* (second edition), chapter 2. The main points are:

1. The limits Claudius sets to worship of himself, with the refusal of a high priest and temples; this follows the policy of Augustus and Tiberius (cf. nos. 3, 4 and 7(b)), and rejected the emphasis of Gaius.

2. His effort at impartial criticism of both Greeks and Jews for the troubles in Alexandria, although coming down rather harder against the Jews.

3. The general interpretation of the civic status of the Jews in Alexandria is that they did *not* possess Alexandrian citizenship.

28   Aureus of Claudius – triumph over the Britons.   AD 46–47

SG 43a = *BMC, Imp.* 1 p. 168, no. 29. *Mint of Rome.*

> *Obverse:* Laureate head of Claudius; around, TI. CLAVD. CAESAR AVG. P.M. TR.P.VI IMP.X.

> *Reverse:* Triumphal arch, surmounted by equestrian statue between two trophies and inscribed DE BRITANN. = *(in record of the triumph)* over the Britons.

The reverse type portrays the arch erected to commemorate Claudius' conquest of Britain (Dio 60.22.1 = LACTOR 11 p.34 and LACTOR 15 pp. 98 and 219); the full inscription on the arch is perhaps SG 43b (see next translation).

29   Claudius, conqueror of British Kings.   AD 51–52

SG 43b = *ILS* 216. *Stone fragments now in the courtyard of the Palazzo dei Conservatori, Capitoline Museum, Rome.*

> To Tiberius Claudius Caesar Augustus Germanicus, son of Drusus, *pontifex maximus*, in the eleventh year of his tribunician power, five times consul, hailed *imperator* twenty-two times, censor, father of his country, the senate and people of Rome *(dedicate this)* because he conquered and received the surrender of eleven British kings without loss and was the first to subject barbarian races beyond the Ocean to the sovereignty of the Roman people.

Probably from Claudius' triumphal arch on the Via Flaminia, Rome. See nos. 28, 35, LACTOR 4 no. 22, and S. S. Frere, *Britannia*[3] 52ff.

30   Career of Quintus Veranius, 45–58.   *c.* AD 58

SG 231c = Gordon, 109. *Last part of Quintus Veranius' tombstone, found about ten kilometres east of Rome.*

> ... he was governor of the province of Lycia with Pamphylia for five years ... he reduced ... to submission to Tiberius Claudius Caesar Augustus Germanicus and stormed and destroyed the fortress of the Cietae Tracheotae; on the written instructions of the senate and people of Rome and of Tiberius Claudius Caesar Augustus Germanicus he completed the restoration of the city walls of Cibyra which had been interrupted ... pacified ... b..
>
> Because of these services, on the proposal of Tiberius Claudius Augustus Germanicus, he was appointed consul and in his consulship he was elected augur on the nomination ... in place of ... nus and was raised to the rank of patrician.
>
> On the decision of Tiberius Claudius Caesar Augustus Germanicus the equestrian class and the Roman people with the agreement of the senate entrusted to him the care of sacred buildings and public works and places.

He was put by the *princeps* Augustus, of whose generosity he was the agent, in charge of the Great Games, so that he might gain the credit for them.

... he was made governor of Britain in which province he died. Verania, daughter of Quintus Veranius, lived six years and ten months.

On Veranius in Britain, see E. Birley, *Britain under Nero* in *Roman Britain and the Roman Army*, 1 ff. His operations in the mountainous area of Cilicia between 45 and 49, when he was consul, are said to have led to his being chosen to conduct campaigns in Wales in 58 (see Tacitus, *Annals* 14. 29 = LACTOR 11 pp. 20 and 69, and *Agricola* 14.3).

31   Two senatorial decrees on building. (a) 22 September AD 45? (b) 2 March AD 56

SG 365 = *ILS* 6043; *FIRA* 1.45. *Bronze tablet from Herculaneum.*

(a)   A decree of the senate on 22 September in the year when Gnaeus Hosidius Geta and Lucius Vagellius were the consuls:

"Since the forethought of our excellent emperor has also looked to the permanence of the buildings of Rome and the whole of Italy, which he himself has aided not only by his most noble command but also by his example; and since it is appropriate to the happiness of the coming age[1] that public and private buildings alike should be protected; and since all men should refrain from that most damaging kind of speculation and should not by destroying houses and villas cause the appearance of Italy to be very unlike that of a country at peace; the senate decrees:

"If any person for the purpose of speculation buys a building with the intention of gaining more by demolishing it than he paid for it, then he shall pay twice the sum at which he bought the property into the treasury, and the matter shall nonetheless be referred to the senate. And since it is equally wrong that selling on the same bad principle should take place, to check vendors too who knowingly and with evil intent sell contrary to this will of the senate, it is decreed that such sales shall be invalid. The senate however asserts that nothing is hereby laid down against those owners who, intending to remain in possession of their own properties, make alterations in parts of them, provided that this is not done for the sake of speculation."

Approved. 383 senators were present.[2]

(b)   A decree of the senate on 2 March in the year when Quintus Volusius and Publius Cornelius were the consuls:

"Because Quintus Volusius and Publius Cornelius spoke on the request of the relatives of Alliatoria Celsilla and asked the senate what it wished done in this matter, the senate decreed on this matter as follows:

"Since the decree of the senate (which was passed on 22 September in the year when Gnaeus Hosidius Geta and Lucius Vagellius, those distinguished senators, were the consuls, on the motion of deified Claudius) forbade anyone to destroy a house or a villa for profit, and forbade anyone

---

[1] Claudius' Secular Games, inaugurating a new era.
[2] Total membership then probably c.600.

for the sake of speculation to buy or sell any property, and established a penalty for the buyer who acted contrary to this decree of the senate, namely that anyone who bought a property should be compelled to pay twice the price of it to the treasury and that the sale should be invalid, but did not change the position of those owners who, intending to remain in possession of their own properties, made alterations in parts of them, only provided that they did not alter them for the sake of speculation;

"And since the relatives of Alliatoria Celsilla, the wife of Atilius Lupercus, the distinguished municipal citizen, explained to this body that her father, Alliatorius Celsus, had bought some land with buildings in the region of Mutina which is called Macer's Fields, where in earlier times a market had regularly been held, but which now for some years had ceased to be held, and these buildings were becoming dilapidated because they were old and would not be repaired for use because nobody lived in them and would not wish to move into empty ruins:

"That Celsilla should not be liable to any damage, fine or penalty if these buildings, which were discussed in this body, should be either destroyed or sold (either by themselves or with the land as well) on the condition that the buyer should be permitted to destroy or remove them without loss to himself. In future, however, others should be advised to refrain from such a disgraceful kind of speculation, especially in this age in which it is more fitting that new buildings should be erected and all of them embellished as a reflection of the prosperity of the world rather than that any part of Italy should be made ugly by the destruction of buildings, and that the irresponsibility of earlier times which had its effect on everything should still be continued so that it could be said that the empire was exhausted with old age ... *(incomplete)*."

Approved. Present ... *(incomplete)*

Cf. Strabo, *Geography* 5.3.7: "They build incessantly because of the collapses and fires and repeated sales, which go on incessantly, too. Indeed, the repeated sales are intentional collapses, so to speak, since they tear down some and build others in their place to their heart's desire."

Note the rhetorical preamble to the first decree and the conclusion to the second. Such expressions of well-meaning paternalism became general in imperial pronouncements, but are particularly noticeable under Claudius, even in senatorial decrees. Concern for the visible signs of prosperity and stability in Rome and Italy is notable, cf. nos. 57, 63, 77–78, 80, 89, 92, 93 and 96; and no. 68 for a similar provision in a Roman town in Spain. The second decree shows how trivial were some of the matters to be decided by the senate.

32   Volubilis receives Roman citizenship.   (a) AD 44; (b) after 54

SG 407 = (a) *CRAI* (1924), pp.77–8;
       (b) *CRAI* (1915), pp.394–7; *FIRA* 1.70.

Volubilis, Mauretania.

(a) To Tiberius Claudius Caesar Augustus Germanicus, son of a god, *pontifex maximus*, holding tribunician power for the fourth time, consul for the third time, consul designate for the fourth time, hailed as *Imperator* for the eighth time, father of his country, the town of Volubilis set up *(this tablet)* by decree of the decurions, when it had gained Roman citizenship, the right of intermarriage, and freedom from compulsory public burdens. Marcus Fadius Celer Flavianus Maximus, imperial procurator with the authority of a legate, dedicated it.

(b) The council of the town of Volubilis *(set up this tablet)* to Marcus Valerius Severus, son of Bostar, of the tribe *Galeria*, aedile, *sufet*, duovir, first priest of the imperial cult of his town, commander of the auxiliary troops against Aedemon who was defeated in the war, because of his services to the state and the success of his mission, when he gained for his fellow-citizens from deified Claudius Roman citizenship, the right of marriage to non-Roman women, freedom from taxation for ten years, the right of including others as residents, and the ownership of the goods of citizens killed in war who had no heirs. *(gap in text)*.

Fabia Bira, the daughter of Izelta, to the kindest of husbands; she accepted the honour but remitted the cost and set it up at her own expense.

Volubilis in Morocco was a Libyan township profoundly influenced by Carthaginian civilisation from the third century BC. It may have been one of the residences of Juba II, Rome's client king of Mauretania under Augustus. The town supported Rome against the revolt of Aedemon after Gaius killed the last king of Mauretania, cf. no. 20, and when the war was finished was appropriately rewarded by Claudius.

In (a) the composer assumes (wrongly) that Claudius must be "son of a god". The title *procurator pro legato* is used of one or two equestrian procurators who temporarily command legionary troops in an emergency.

In (b) the name Bostar is Carthaginian, as is the title *sufet*, or "chief magistrate"; Bira and Izelta are Libyan. For another *sufet*, see no. 19.

See A. Momigliano, *Claudius* (second edition) 66ff. and A. N. Sherwin-White, *The Roman Citizenship* 181ff. for these texts and Claudius' grants of Roman citizenship, and cf. next item.

33   Claudius settles disputed claims to Roman citizenship.   AD 46

SG 368 = *ILS* 206; *FIRA* 1.71. *Bronze tablet, found in Val di Non, near Trento, in 1869; now in Trento.*

On 15 March in the consulship of Marcus Junius Silanus and Quintus Sulpicius Camerinus the edict of Tiberius Claudius Caesar Augustus Germanicus which is written below was published at the imperial residence at Baiae.

Tiberius Claudius Caesar Augustus Germanicus, *pontifex maximus*, holding the tribunician power for the sixth time, hailed as *Imperator* eleven times, father of his country, designated to be consul for the fourth time, declares:

"Arising out of the old disputes which had been in existence for some time even in the reign of my uncle, Tiberius Caesar, to settle which disputes (which concerned only the people of Comum, as far as I remember, and the Bergaleians) he sent Pinarius Apollinaris, and he, first because of the prolonged absence of my uncle from Rome and then in the reign of Gaius, too, because he was not required to make a report, had not (wisely indeed) done so, it has latterly been shown to me by Camurius Statutus that a considerable part of the fields and woodland are under my jurisdiction. So I have sent Julius Planta, my friend and associate, to deal with this matter. After he summoned my procurators both of other areas and of that neighbourhood, he has investigated the matter with the greatest care and discovered the details. These therefore, as explained to me in the report which he has made, he will decide and pronounce on with my permission *(gap in text)*

"As far as this concerns the status of the Anaunians,[1] the Tulliassians[1] and the Sindunians,[1] some of whom an informer is said to have proved to have been only annexed[2] to the Tridentines, and some of them not even annexed, although I note that this class of persons does not have a very strong claim to Roman citizenship, nevertheless, since they are said to have been in possession of it for a long time and to be so intermingled with the Tridentines that they could not be separated from them without serious harm to that distinguished city, I permit them to retain that right which they believed they had. I do this the more willingly because I am told that a good number of this class of persons is serving in my praetorian guard, some indeed as centurions, and that some of them have been appointed to juries in Rome and decide lawsuits.

"I grant this favour to them on condition that whatever they have done and transacted as if they were Roman citizens either among themselves or with the Tridentines or other people should on my authority stand; and with my permission they may retain the names which they used before as if they had been Roman citizens."

In the first part there is evidence of the slowness with which the administrative machine worked if the emperor for any reason was not available – in this case, Tiberius in seclusion on Capri.

In the second part Claudius determines that strict legality would be administratively impossible, and that in any case good service to the Roman state justifies his action. See no. 32 and note.

34   Claudius addresses the Senate.   AD 48

SG 369 = *ILS* 212; *FIRA* 1.43. *Bronze tablet found at Lyons in* 1528; *now in Lyons Museum.*

(1.1 *fragmentary*) "I beg you first of all not to show the common reaction people have to new proposals, a reaction which I can already see will be the very first obstacle to my proposal, which is to be horrified at it as though it were something unprecedented. I ask you rather to consider how many innovations have been made in this state, how many different forms of constitution have been established in our country (right from the foundation of Rome). *(gap in text)*

[1] Modern Non, Dolas, Saône.
[2] I.e. they were subject to its jurisdiction without enjoying full civic rights.

"In ancient times kings governed this city, but they were not lucky enough to have as successors members of their own families. Other families took over power, sometimes even foreigners. Examples of this are Numa, Romulus's successor, who was a Sabine, a neighbouring people indeed but not at that time part of the Roman state, and Tarquinius Priscus who came after Ancus Martius. He was refused any opportunity of winning an honourable position in Tarquinii (*Trachina*) because of his tainted family background: his father, Demarathus, was a Corinthian, and his mother, although a Tarquinian, came from a good family that was impoverished and so had no option but to marry such a husband. But after coming to Rome he gained the throne.

"Between the first Tarquin and his son (or grandson – for this, too, is reported differently by different authors) came Servius Tullius. He was the son of a woman prisoner of war, Ocresia, according to Roman authors. Etruscan writers maintain that originally he was the most loyal of Caelius Vivenna's companions, who had been with him in all his adventures. Forced to leave Etruria after various escapades with all that was left of Caelius's army, he seized the Caelian Mount, so named after his own leader. At the same time he changed his own name, which in Tuscan had been Mastarna, to Servius Tullius, as I have mentioned. And his reign was of the greatest benefit to the state.

"Next came Tarquin the Proud, but his behaviour (and that of his sons equally) became so intolerable to the citizens of Rome that public opinion was thoroughly disgusted with the monarchy. The government was therefore entrusted to consuls, magistrates elected annually. *(gap in text)*

"I don't need to refer now to the dictatorial powers, established by our ancestors to be more embracing than those of the consuls, which were called into operation in times of more than usual crisis whether in external wars or in civil disturbances. Nor to the plebeian tribunes, appointed to help ordinary citizens. Nor to the transference of supreme power from the consuls to the decemvirs, and then back again to the consuls after the reign of the decemvirs had been brought to an end. Nor, further, to the fact that consular power was divided among a larger number of men, the military tribunes with consular authority, who were appointed six and often eight each year. Nor finally to the sharing by plebeians in the priesthoods as well as in positions of secular power.

"If I were now to speak of the wars by which our ancestors first established their power and the point we have now advanced to, I fear I should seem too arrogant. You would think I was trying to boast of the honour of extending our Empire beyond the Ocean. But I shall go back rather to the point that the citizenship ... *(rest of this paragraph lost)*

(gap in text) "... can be. It was, of course, an innovation when both my great-uncle, deified Augustus, and my uncle, Tiberius Caesar, wanted to have all the best men from colonies and municipalities everywhere in this senate, provided they had the necessary qualifications of character and wealth. You may object that an Italian senator is preferable to a provincial one. Well, I soon shall make clear my opinion on this when I begin to ask for your approval on that part of my censorship. But in my opinion

not even provincials should be rejected if they can be of value to the senate.

"Remember, I beg you, for how many years now senators have come to this body from the distinguished and wealthy colony of Vienne. From this colony has come Lucius Vestinus,[1] that excellent and outstanding member of the equestrian order, whom I number among my closest friends and whom today I am employing in my private affairs. And I beg that his children may enjoy the first rank of the priesthoods and later, as the years go by, advance to further honours in their position. I shall not mention the ill-omened name of a certain rogue.[2] I dislike intensely that monstrosity of the wrestling ring who brought the consulship into his family before his home town had received the full benefit of the Roman citizenship. I could say the same about his brother who, because of this very unfortunate and disgraceful circumstance cannot be a useful member of the senate. *(gap in text)*

"Now is the time, Tiberius Caesar Germanicus,[3] to reveal to the members of this house the purport of your speech; for you have already reached the extreme edge of Narbonese Gaul. *(gap in text)*

"All those noble young men whom I am looking at would cause us no more embarrassment if they became senators than my friend Persicus,[4] that most aristocratic of men, is embarrassed by reading the name of Allobrogicus[5] among the busts of his ancestors. If this is so, what further argument do you want, when I point out that the hinterland itself beyond the frontiers of Narbonese Gaul is already sending us senators? For we have senators from Lyons whom we are glad to welcome into our order. I am apprehensive, gentlemen, of going beyond the frontiers you are accustomed to and familiar with; but the case of Gallia Comata must now be argued. If anyone is concerned about the fact that the people there plagued deified Julius for ten years in war, let him set against that a hundred years of resolute loyalty, an allegiance which has more than stood the test of many difficult crises in the Empire. It was they who ensured that my father Drusus, when he was engaged in the conquest of Germany, had behind him a province that was safe, quiet, reliable and peaceful, even though he was called away to the war while conducting the census, which was something new and unaccustomed for the Gauls. The difficulty of this task we are at this time particularly discovering ourselves by all too bitter experience, although we are trying merely to publish the state of our resources." *(gap in text)*

One of the most discussed Roman inscriptions, containing part of a speech of Claudius with which we can compare Tacitus' version in *Annals* 11.23–25 (see K. Wellesley, *Greece and Rome* 1954, 13–33 on this point). On the question of the admission of Gauls to the senate, cf. A. Momigliano, *Claudius*

---

[1] A member of the imperial council and prefect of Egypt under Nero (cf. no. 50).
[2] Valerius Asiaticus, forced to commit suicide in 47 after conviction.
[3] Claudius addressing himself.
[4] Paullus Fabius Persicus, member of the imperial council, consul in 34, proconsul of Asia between 51 and 54.
[5] Quintus Fabius Maximus Allobrogicus, consul in 121 BC, defeated the Arverni and Allobroges on 8 August 121 BC (cf. Pliny, *Natural History* 7.166).

chapter 3 and A. N. Sherwin-White, *The Roman Citizenship*, 181ff. It may be noted that in fact extremely few Gauls entered the senate under Claudius or later, perhaps either because the emperors felt mistrustful after the events of 68–71, or because Gallic notables subsequently lacked interest or were otherwise unsuitable.

35 Members of Claudius' family. AD 51–52

SG 100 = *ILS* 222; Gordon 103. *Stone from the Campus Martius, Rome.*

(1) To Germanicus Caesar, son of Tiberius Augustus, grandson of deified Augustus, great-grandson of deified Julius, augur, *flamen* of Augustus, twice consul, twice hailed as *Imperator*.

(2) To Antonia Augusta, wife of Drusus, priestess of deified Augustus, mother of Tiberius Claudius Caesar Augustus, father of his country.

(3) To Julia Augusta Agrippina, daughter of Germanicus Caesar, wife of Tiberius Claudius Caesar Augustus, father of his country.

(4) To Nero Claudius Caesar Drusus Germanicus, son of [Claudius] Augustus, *pontifex*, augur, member of the board of fifteen in charge of religious rites and of the board of seven in charge of sacrificial feasts, consul designate, leader of the youth.

(5) To Octavia, daughter of Tiberius Claudius Caesar Augustus, father of his country.

Inscriptions in five columns, probably accompanying statues of members of Claudius' family adorning his triumphal arch (see no. 29). They are Germanicus, Antonia Minor, Agrippina the Younger, Nero, and Octavia, daughter of Claudius and Messalina and later wife of Nero. It was important for Claudius because of his background to emphasise his connexion with the Julian family. Note the honours already enjoyed by Nero, though he is only about fourteen years old.

The digamma is used in this inscription, one of the letters introduced into the alphabet by Claudius (cf. Tacitus, *Annals* 11.13–14).

36 A Greek's equestrian career under Claudius and Nero.

SG 262 = *IGRR* 4.1086; *SIG*³ 804. *Stone from Cos.*

(The people of Cos honour) Gaius Stertinius Xenophon, son of Heraclitus, of the tribe *Cornelia*, chief physician to the divine Augusti and in charge of Greek correspondence; he had been military tribune and "prefect of engineers" and was decorated with a golden crown and spear in the triumph over the Britons; son of his people, devoted friend of Nero,[1] of Caesar, of Augustus, of Rome, of his city, benefactor of his city, chief priest of the gods and priest for life of the Augusti and of Asclepius and of Hygeia and of Epione; *(erected)* when Marcus Septicius Rufus, son of Marcus, and Ariston, son of Philocles, devoted friends of the Caesars, were temple treasurers.

---

[1] Engraved over an erasure of "devoted friend of Claudius" after Claudius' death and subsequently itself erased.

The emperor Claudius granted exemption from taxation to the people of Cos, on the petition of Xenophon, who was a native of the island and Claudius' own doctor (Tacitus, *Annals* 12.61.2.) Later, according to Tacitus (*Annals* 12.67.2–4), he was called in to assist in Claudius' murder. See Pliny, *Natural History* 29.7 for his vast wealth. One of several Greeks who followed equestrian careers as early as the reigns of Claudius and Nero.

(d) NERO

37 The Career of Burrus.

SG 259 = *ILS* 1321. *Stone from Vaison* (Vasio) *in Narbonese Gaul.*

> The Vocontii of Vaison *(set this up)* in honour of their patron Sextus Afranius Burrus, son of Sextus, of the tribe *Voltinia*, military tribune, procurator of the empress, procurator of Tiberius Caesar, procurator of deified Claudius, prefect of the Praetorian Guard, honoured with the insignia of a consul.

Burrus was appointed praetorian prefect by Claudius in 51 and continued under Nero until his death in 62. Although Tacitus (*Annals* 12.42) praises his military reputation, his early career was largely civilian as financial agent of Livia (who died in 29) (see nos. 2–4, 7(b) and 21), Tiberius and Claudius. He appears to have been a native of Vaison. For other patrons see no. 19 *note*.

38 Julius Classicianus, procurator of Britain.   *c*. AD 61–64

SG 268 = *RIB* 12. *Stone found partly in 1852, partly in 1935 in Roman wall, London; now in British Museum.*

> To the spirits of the departed and of Gaius Julius Alpinus Classicianus, son of Gaius, of the tribe *Fabia*, … procurator of the province of Britain; Julia Pacata I[ndiana?], his wife, daughter of Indus, *(set this up)*.

In 61 Classicianus succeeded Decianus Catus as procurator of Britain after the Boudican revolt. By direct appeal to the emperor he was instrumental in securing the recall and replacement of Suetonius Paulinus, who had crushed the revolt, by a less aggressive governor. Classicianus, himself a provincial from Gaul, had married the daughter of a Treveran Gaul, Indus, who (according to Tacitus, *Annals* 3.42) had actively opposed the Gallic rebellion under Florus in 21. See S. S. Frere, *Britannia*³ 74, and LACTOR 4, no. 24.

39 Semis of Nero: Neronian Games.   AD 64–66

SG 57 = *BMC, Imp.* 1, p.251, no.261. *Mint of Rome.*

> *Obverse:* Laureate head of Nero; around, NERO CAES. AVG. IMP.

> *Reverse:* Table with urn and wreath; above, S[EMIS]; on either side, S C; around, CER[TAMEN] QVINQ[VENNALE] ROM[AE] CO[NSTITVTVM] = quinquennial contest established at Rome.

The reverse type refers to the games founded by Nero in 60 and celebrated for a second time in 65; the wreath is for the victor, the urn for the votes of the judges. The games, popularly known as *Neronia*, were in the Greek style, including competitions in poetry and rhetoric as well as athletics. Nero took part personally in 65. Cf. nos. 40 and 72.

40   As of Nero: Nero and Apollo.   AD 64–66

SG 144 = *BMC, Imp.* 1, p.250, no.257. *Mint of Rome.*

> *Obverse:* Radiate head of Nero; around, NERO CLAVD. CAESAR AVG. GERMANIC.
>
> *Reverse:* Apollo playing lyre; around, PONTIF. MAX. TR. POT. IMP. P.P.

The titulature runs continuously from obverse to reverse; the radiate crown, symbol of divinity, appears in the Roman coinage on the head of a living emperor for the first time under Nero. Nero is identified with Apollo Citharoedus (Apollo the lyre player). This is so exceptional that it was noted by Suetonius (*Nero* 25) in one of the very few references to coin types in ancient literature. Cf. no. 41.

See previous item for another example of Nero's artistic pursuits.

41   Nero the new Apollo.

SG 145 = *IG* 2/3², 3278. *Stone from Athens.*

> To the emperor Nero Caesar Augustus the new Apollo.

In the course of his principate Nero was increasingly identified with several of the Olympian gods – with Zeus and Helios at Acraephia (no. 46), with Hercules at Rome (Suetonius, *Nero* 53) and according to Dio 61.20.5, he was acclaimed as Nero-Apollo by senators on his return from Greece. In this Greek inscription he is equated with Apollo. Cf. no. 40.

42   The Danube frontier and the Chersonese.   After AD 74

SG 228 = *ILS* 986. *Stone near Tibur, by the mausoleum of the Plautii.*

> To Tiberius Plautius Silvanus Aelianus, son of Marcus, of the tribe *Aniensis, pontifex,* priest of Augustus, one of the board of three directors of the Mint, quaestor of Tiberius Caesar, legate of the fifth legion in Germany, praetor urbanus, legate and member of the staff of Claudius Caesar in Britain, consul, proconsul of Asia, propraetorian legate of Moesia, in which he transported more than 100,000 of the Trans-Danubians with their wives and children and chiefs and kings to be tribute-paying subjects; he crushed a rising of Sarmatians at its outset, although he had despatched a large part of his army to the expedition against Armenia; he transported kings hitherto unknown and hostile to the Roman People to the river bank which he was guarding to pay homage to the Roman standards; he restored their sons to the kings of the Bastarnae and Rhoxolani, and to the king of the Dacians his brothers, who had been rescued or captured from the enemy; from some of them he took hostages;

by these means he both assured and extended the peace of the province,
driving the king of the Scythians from the siege of Heraclea of the
Chersonese, which lies beyond the Dnieper; he was the first to add to the
corn-supply of the Roman People with a large amount of wheat from that
province; while legate in Spain he was recalled to hold the urban prefecture, and in his prefecture the Senate honoured him with triumphal
decorations, at the instigation of the emperor Caesar Augustus Vespasian
in words from his speech which are quoted below:

"He governed Moesia so well that the honour of his triumphal decorations should not have been deferred to my time, except that by the delay
a more distinguished title fell to his lot as urban prefect."

While holding the same urban prefecture the emperor Caesar Augustus
Vespasian conferred upon him a second consulship.

A very complete account of a Senatorial career, covering at least five princi-
pates from Tiberius to Vespasian and including an unusually detailed description
of one particular stage of that career. Plautius was consul in 45 and 74.

See B. H. Warmington, *Nero* 84 for the activity on the Danube frontier and
in the Chersonese *c*. 62. Probably no major battles took place or they would
have been mentioned on Plautius' inscription, but it is surprising that these
events are not mentioned by Tacitus. In spite of them, the Sarmatians, Dacians
and Rhoxolani became a formidable threat to the Roman position under the
Flavians: cf. nos. 70 and 71.

43   Nero's policy in the East.   AD 64–65

SG 51b = *ILS* 232. *Stone from Charput (Ziata?), Armenia.*

Nero Claudius Caesar Augustus Germanicus, emperor, *pontifex maximus*,
in the eleventh year of his tribunician power, four times consul, hailed as
Imperator nine times, father of his country *(set this up)* by the hand of
Gnaeus Domitius Corbulo, imperial propraetorian legate, and Titus
Aurelius Fulvus, legate of the third legion *Gallica*.

See B. H. Warmington, *Nero* 85–100 for Nero's policy in the East, and the
campaigns of Corbulo. Although a preliminary agreement was reached in 63
whereby Rome would recognise Tiridates as king of Armenia, this inscription
shows that Roman troops remained there probably at least till Tiridates' visit
to Rome in 66. See no. 44.

44   Sestertius of Nero: Nero closes the temple of Janus.   AD 64–65

SG 53 = *BMC, Imp.* 1, p.214, note*.

Obverse: Laureate bust of Nero; around, NERO CLAVD. CAES. AVG.
IMP. TR. POT. XI P.P.

Reverse: Temple of Janus, with door closed; on either side, S C; around,
PACE P[OPVLO] R[OMANO] TERRA MARIQ[VE] PARTA IANVM
CLVSIT = (Nero), after establishing peace on land and sea for the Roman
people, closed the temple of Janus.

The temple of Janus was closed after the settlement of the Armenian question (Suetonius, *Nero* 13) in 63 and perhaps again in 66 when Tiridates of Armenia came to Rome in person. This ceremony, symbolising peace everywhere, had not been performed since the time of Augustus who closed the temple three times. See no. 43.

45 Scribonius Proculus. Probably AD 66

SG 160 = *ILS* 9235. (a) *Stone base of a column bearing the statue of Jupiter, Mainz (Moguntiacum).* (b) *On an adjacent altar.*

> (a) To Jupiter Best and Greatest for the safety of Nero[1] Claudius Caesar Augustus, emperor, the inhabitants of the civil settlement *(dedicated this)* as a public monument when Publius Sulpicius Scribonius Proculus was imperial propraetorian legate, under the care and at the expense of Quintus Julius Priscus and Quintus Julius Auctus.
>
> *(on the side of the monument)*
> Samus and Severus, sons of Venicarius, were the sculptors.
>
> (b) To Jupiter Best and Greatest, Quintus Julius Priscus and Quintus Julius Auctus *(dedicated this)*.

Scribonius Proculus and his brother Scribonius Rufus, governors of Lower and Upper Germany respectively, were among those forced to commit suicide *c.*66. This may have been connected with the failure of the Vinician conspiracy, but a number of the old nobility fell victim about the same time.

The dedicants are Roman citizens, although doubtless Gauls, but the artists are not. The monument is the so-called Jupiter column of Mainz.

46 Nero "frees" Achaea. 28 November AD 67

SG 64 = *ILS* 8794; *SIG*³ 814. *Stone from Karditza (Acraephia), Boeotia.*

> The Emperor Caesar says: "Wishing to requite the noblest land of Hellas for her goodwill and respect towards me I order as many as possible from this province to be present at Corinth on the 28th day of November."
> When the crowds came together in the assembly he addressed them in the following words:
> "It is an unexpected gift, Hellenes, that I grant you – although nothing is beyond expectation from my generosity – a gift so great that you were incapable of asking for it. All you Hellenes, who inhabit Achaea and what was till now the Peloponnese, receive your freedom and immunity from taxation which you did not enjoy even in your most fortunate days. For you were enslaved either to foreigners or to one another. I wish that I were offering this gift when Hellas was in its heyday, so that more might benefit from my favour. For this reason I blame time for squandering already the extent of my favour. Even now it is not through pity

---

[1] Erased.

so much as goodwill that I grant this benefit to you, and I make a requital to your gods, whose consideration for me I have always experienced both by land and sea, because they have allowed me to bestow so great a favour. Other leaders have liberated cities, Nero alone has liberated a province."

Epaminondas, son of Epaminondas, high priest of the Augusti for life and of Nero Claudius Caesar Augustus, spoke as follows, declaring that he had proposed this decree to the council and people.

"Since Nero, lord of the whole world, mightiest emperor, in the thirteenth year of his tribunician power, father of his country, new Hêlios shining upon the Hellenes, having chosen to show kindness to Hellas and at the same time requiting and reverencing our gods for always standing by him in providence and protection, since he alone throughout all time mightiest emperor, philhellene, Nero Zeus god of Freedom, has given, granted and re-established in its ancient state of autonomy the freedom of the Hellenes indigenous and innate from all time which had formerly been removed, granting in addition to this great, unexpected gift immunity from taxation, which no one of the former Augusti granted in full, for all these reasons it has been decided by rulers and councillors and people to dedicate at this present time the altar to Zeus the Saviour with the inscription

To Zeus god of Freedom Nero for ever

and to set up alongside our own native gods in the temple of Apollo Ptôïos statues of Nero Zeus god of Freedom and divine Augusta Messalina, so that when this work is completed our city also may be seen to have rendered in full all honour and reverence to the house of Nero lord Augustus. And it is proposed that the decree be inscribed on a block of stone alongside the temple of Zeus the Saviour in the market-place and on the temple of Apollo Ptôïos ."

This famous inscription refers to Nero's grant of "freedom" to the province of Achaea in 67, the climax of his visit to Greece and his philhellene policy (cf. nos. 39–41). The authentic voice of Nero may be detected in the first part, and the propensity of the eastern communities to worship living emperors in the second (cf. nos. 5 and 27). The Greeks appear to have been genuinely enthusiastic for Nero, though this was of no assistance to him in Rome. The grant of freedom was cancelled by Vespasian.

47   Coins: Anti-Neronian sentiments in Gaul.   AD 68

SG 70. *Mint or mints in Gaul.*

(a) Denarius, *BMC, Imp.* 1, p.297, no.31.

Obverse: Victory holding wreath and palm; around, SALVS GENERIS HVMANI = the salvation of the human race.

Reverse: S[ENATVS] P[OPVLVS]Q[VE] R[OMANVS] = the senate and people of Rome.

(b) Aureus, *BMC, Imp.* 1, p.299, no.38.

Obverse: Bust of Mars; around, MARS VLTOR = Mars the avenger.

Reverse: Legionary eagle and altar between two standards; below, SIGNA P[OPVLI] R[OMANI] = the standards of the Roman people.

(c) Denarius, *BMC, Imp.* 1, p.294, note*.

Obverse: Bust of Hercules; around, HERCVLES ADSERTOR = Hercules the protector.

Reverse: Fortuna holding wreath and cornucopiae; around, FLORENTE FORTVNA P[OPVLI] R[OMANI] = at a time when the Fortune of the people of Rome is prospering.

(d) Denarius, *BMC, Imp.* 1, p.295, no.19.

Obverse: Helmeted bust of Roma; around, ROMA RESTITVTA = with Rome restored.

Reverse: Jupiter seated, holding sceptre and thunderbolt; around, IVPPITER LIBERATOR = Jupiter the Liberator.

Coins of Vindex and, possibly, Galba. The slogans are calculated to appeal to "Republican", i.e. anti-Neronian sentiments.

In a letter to Galba (Suetonius, *Galba*, 9), Vindex asked him to be the "champion of the human race" (cf. (a)). The reverse of (a) is in line with Galba's refusal to consider himself as emperor till proclaimed at Rome.

(b) Mars Ultor no doubt refers to the prospect of vengeance of Nero's crimes, and the reverse is patriotic.

(c) Hercules was very popular in the Gallic provinces.

(d) The appeal for the restoration of Rome is matched by the symbol of Jupiter the Liberator.

48   Epitaph of Verginius Rufus.

MW 531.

Not in existence as an inscription but quoted by Pliny (*Letters* 6.10) where he complains that nine years after his death Rufus' tomb is not yet finished and is without name or inscription.

> "Here lies Rufus who defeated Vindex and then refused the throne for himself but claimed it for his country."

Pliny repeats the epitaph in *Letters* 9.19, and tells us that Rufus composed it for himself.

Lucius Verginius Rufus, governor of Upper Germany under Nero, put down the rising of Julius Vindex in Gaul at Vesontio in 68, after some delay. Some time after the battle and Vindex's suicide – the chronology is obscure – Rufus' troops offered him the throne which he refused, possibly because he thought he was unsuitable being the son of an *eques*. See P. A. Brunt, *Latomus* 18 (1959) 531–559.

II. YEAR OF FOUR EMPERORS

(a) GALBA

49   A supporter of Galba.   AD 109–110

MW 31 = *IRT* 537. *Limestone blocks from the Arch of Trajan at Lepcis Magna,* *still* in situ.

> Quintus Pomponius Rufus, consul, *pontifex*, member of the Flavian brotherhood, commissioner for public works, imperial propraetorian legate of the provinces of Moesia, Dalmatia and Spain, commander of the fifth legion, prefect of the sea coast of nearer Spain and Gallia Narbonensis in the war which the emperor Galba fought on behalf of the state, proconsul of the province of Africa, through the agency of Lucius Asinius Rufus, propraetorian legate ...

Quintus Pomponius Rufus was presumably a junior officer in Spain at the time of Galba's bid for the throne in 68 and, as a commander of the naval forces supporting and protecting Galba's right flank, must have played an important part in it. The reference to Galba's campaign is unique in inscriptions. It is remarkable that Rufus' subsequent career under the Flavians was quite exceptionally slow, as he did not reach the consulship till 95 and the proconsulate of Africa under Trajan in 109 or 110. The *Sodales Flaviales* were a priestly brotherhood (cf. the Arval Brotherhood, no. 69) founded to honour the Flavian dynasty.

50   Edict of Tiberius Julius Alexander.   6 July AD 68

SG 391 (MW 328) = *IGRR* 1.1263; *OGIS* 669; *FIRA* 1.58; revised text *SEG* 16.861.
> *El-Khargeh Oasis, Egypt, on the outer gateway of the temple of Hibis.*

> Julius Demetrius, controller *(stratêgos)* of the nome of the Thebaid Oasis: "I publish this copy of the edict of the lord prefect Tiberius Julius Alexander which has been sent to me so that you may know and be glad of his good services towards you." Dated 1 Phaoph, a Julian Augustan day, in the second year of the emperor Lucius Livius Augustus Sulpicius Galba. *(28 September 68)*.
>   Tiberius Julius Alexander proclaims: "Since I am very eager that the city *(of Alexandria)* should continue to have the status that befits it, enjoying the privileges which it has received from the emperors; and also that Egypt should remain stable, ungrudgingly upholding the wealth and very great prosperity of the present time, and not burdened by new and unjust exactions; and since almost from the day I entered the city I have been faced with an outcry from those I have met both in small groups and large who are the most decent citizens in Alexandria or who farm outside it, all of whom complain about recent abuses; I have not rested from doing everything in my power to correct what has been pressed on my attention. And so that you may with the greater cheerfulness repose every hope of both

rescue and happiness in the beneficence of the emperor Augustus Galba, who has appeared as a light of salvation in our times for the safety of all mankind; and so that you may know that I have given thought to what conduces to helping you, I have of necessity published my decisions in each of the requests made to me, where I have the authority to judge and act. Those cases that are more grave and require the authority and majesty of the emperor I shall send on to him, stating the facts in complete truth. For the gods have kept the security of the whole world safe to this most sacred time.

1   "I know that the most reasonable by far of all your petitions is that unwilling persons should not be forced into tax-collection or the leasing of imperial property, contrary to the usual practice of the provinces. I am aware that the fact that inexperienced people are pressed into service has damaged the economy severely, since tax-collection is thrust upon them of necessity. For this reason I myself have not made anyone a tax-collector or a lessee of imperial property, nor shall I do so, because I realise that to have capable volunteers doing this job zealously is of benefit to the imperial accounts. I am convinced that no one in the future will be made a tax-collector or a lessee of imperial property contrary to his wish; the posts will instead be given to those who offer themselves, because it is better to continue the established custom of previous governors than to imitate a short-lived injustice.

2   "Since some people, using public debts as an excuse, have had the loans of others conceded to them and have consigned their victims to the debtors' prison and other prisons which I know have been abolished for this very reason, that exactions of debt might be made on the property and not on the persons of the debtors; following the wish of deified Augustus, I give orders that nobody on excuse of public debts shall have loans of others conceded to him which he did not himself make in the first place, and that no free citizen under any circumstances shall be put into any prison whatsoever, unless he is a criminal, nor into the debtors' prison, apart from those who are in debt to the imperial treasury.

3   "To prevent state business being used as an excuse for undermining agreements between individuals, and to stop creditors who misuse the right of first payment affecting public confidence, I have of necessity promulgated a decree on this, too: I have been often told that some people have already tried to take away deposits lawfully made and to exact by force repaid loans from those who have received them and to reverse purchases, taking the goods away from the buyers on the grounds that they had made an agreement with people who had unpaid debts owing to the imperial treasury, such as military personnel, civil servants or others who owed money to a public account. So I instruct all procurators of the emperor and administrators in Egypt, if they are suspicious of any person who is employed in state business, to keep a record of his name or to post it in public, to prevent anyone lending money to him, or to keep some of his property in the public record-boxes for debt. If anyone whose name has not been noted or for whom security has not been taken lends money

lawfully on deposit, or if he takes his money back early or if he buys something with it, provided his name has not been taken nor his property secured, he will have no trouble. For both deified Augustus and the prefects of Egypt have decreed that gifts which are the property of other people and not of the debtors should be repaid from the imperial treasury to their wives, whose right to first payment must be carefully maintained.

4   "I have met requests, too, concerning freedom from taxation and partial remission of taxes, including public revenue, where the petitioners ask that these privileges be safeguarded, following the exemptions granted by deified Claudius in a letter to Postumus; they also claim that afterwards payments were exacted by private individuals in the time between Flaccus's original assessment and the exemption granted by deified Claudius. Since therefore both Balbillus and Vestinus granted these exemptions, I confirm the edicts of both prefects, who themselves followed the favour granted by deified Claudius, so that the petitioners are exempted from paying what has never yet been demanded, and clearly their exemption or reduction will be maintained in future.

5   "With reference to the policies followed on Caesar's advice in the interim period, where land-tax was imposed, Vestinus decreed that the appropriate tax should be paid, and I confirm it, remitting what has not yet been exacted, and declare for the future the tax to remain as appropriate. For it is unjust that those who bought property and paid its value should be asked to pay rent on their own property as though they were farming public land.

6   "It is also in accordance with the privileges granted by the emperors that native-born Alexandrians who go to live in the country to work should not be liable to any rural public service. You have requested this many times, and I confirm that no native-born Alexandrian shall be liable to any rural public service.

7   "It will also be my responsibility to arrange after the assizes that the post of controller of the nome will be tenable for three years by those appointed.

8   "I make a universal edict that, whenever a prefect has judged a case brought before him and acquitted the defendant, the case must not again be brought to court. If two prefects give the same judgement on a case, the accountant who brought the same case is to be punished, since he is doing nothing else than giving an excuse for money-making to himself and the other civil servants. Many people, I know, have decided instead to abandon their property because they have spent more than its value through the same case coming to court at each assizes.

9   "I establish the same rule for cases brought under the special account, too. If therefore any case has been discussed and dismissed by the judge in the special account court, it will no longer be permitted to this prosecutor to arraign anyone or bring a case to court; if he does, he will be punished most severely. For there will be no end of false accusations, if dismissed cases are brought up until somebody finds for the prosecution.

Because of the large number of informers, the city has already become almost depopulated and every home disturbed. I therefore of necessity order that, if anyone prosecutes in the court of the special account on someone else's behalf, he must produce the real prosecutor in court, so that he too may not be free from risk. If he brings three prosecutions under his own name unsuccessfully, he shall no longer be allowed to prosecute and half his property shall be confiscated. For it is very unjust that the man who endangers the property or citizenship of many other people should himself have complete immunity. In general I shall order that the regulations of the special account be confirmed, since I have corrected the innovations brought in contrary to the privileges granted by the emperors. I shall clearly proclaim how I have duly punished those already found guilty of malicious accusation.

10   "I am well aware that you are very anxious that Egypt continue to be prosperous, although this prosperity causes you hardship. As far as public obligations are concerned, I have corrected them as far as I can. For I have frequently met farmers from all over the country who have told me that many new demands have been imposed on them, not because of any fraud, but because of tax assessments in corn and money, even though it was not lawful for anyone who liked rashly to introduce innovations of universal application. These and similar demands I have found being made not only in the Thebaid or the districts far away from Lower Egypt; they have already reached the suburbs of the city, the so-called Hinterland of Alexandria, and the Mareotic area. I therefore order the administrators of each nome to restore the earlier tax-rate, if any change in taxation on farmers has been made in the last five years which has not been either universal or common to many districts and areas. They should not demand payment of these new taxes, and I too shall dismiss these demands if they are brought to my assizes.

11   "I have checked the excessive power of the public accountants even before this because of the general outcry against them for making most of the entries in the tax registers by analogy. The result of this has been that they have become rich but Egypt ruined. Now again I proclaim to them that they must not enter anything by analogy nor do anything else without a decision from the prefect. I also order the administrators not to accept any ruling from the public accountants without a direction from the prefect. If other civil servants too are found guilty of false or unnecessary entries in public records, they will repay the individual what they have robbed him of and pay an equal amount to the treasury.

12   "Another example of the same falsification is the so-called tax-demand by average. This is based not on the actual rising of the Nile, although nothing seems more just than the true height, but on an average of various earlier risings. It is my wish that men should farm the land gladly and willingly, knowing that tax-demands will be based on the true and current rising and extent of inundation, not on the deception of demand by average. A man convicted of falsifying these facts will pay back three times what he stole.

13   "Those who have been apprehensive when they heard of the surveying
       of the land anciently part of Alexandria and the Menelaitic nome, where
       never before has any measuring tape been brought, need not be on their
       guard. For no one has ever dared or ever will dare to do a survey there.
       The ancient rights of that area must remain inviolate.

14   "I decree the same regulations too about the areas added to these, so
       that no innovation with regard to them be made.

15   "With regard to longer-standing cases in which you are involved, which
       some of you began in the hope they would finally define your liabilities,
       but which often achieved nothing more than profit for the civil servants
       and loss to you, I shall refer these to the emperor Caesar Augustus, with
       all the other things I send to him, who alone has the power to end such
       nuisances completely, and whose beneficence and concern are the causes
       of security for us all."

       Dated 12 Epiphi in the first year of the Emperor Lucius Livius Galba
       Caesar Augustus. *(6 July 68)*.

This famous inscription was issued so soon after the fall of Nero that it has
been suggested that Alexander knew in advance of the project of Vindex and
Galba. Allowing for the propagandist element in favour of Galba in the preamble (cf. no. 47), the inscription seems to indicate that the administration of Egypt
under Nero had been forced to indulge in various abuses of power under the
pressure of Nero's demands for revenue.

Egypt was divided for administrative purposes into nomes, each controlled
by a *stratêgos*. See A. H. M. Jones, *Cities of the Eastern Roman Provinces*, 295.

(b) OTHO

51   Edict of the proconsul of Sardinia.   18 March AD 69

SG 392 = MW 455 = *ILS* 5947; *FIRA* 1.59. *Esterzili, Sardinia*.

In the consulship of the emperor Otho Caesar Augustus, on 18 March,
this was copied from and checked against the bound book of Lucius
Helvius Agrippa, the proconsul, which Gnaeus Egnatius Fuscus, the
quaestor's clerk, published. In this was written what is written below in
list 5, sections 8–10.

On 13 March, Lucius Helvius Agrippa, the proconsul, heard the case
and pronounced as his judgement: "Since it is to the public good that decisions at law once made should stand; and since Marcus Juventius Rixa,
the distinguished imperial procurator, has frequently given his judgement
in the case of the people of Patulcum that 'the boundaries of the people
of Patulcum should be kept as they were laid down by Marcus Metellus
and inscribed on a bronze tablet', and finally ordained that 'he had intended
to punish the people of Gallilum because they constantly renewed the argument and refused to obey his decree; but out of respect for the clemency
of the great and good emperor he thought it enough to warn them by edict
that they should keep the peace, should abide by the decision already

reached and should by 1 October next leave the lands of the people of Patulcum and hand over vacant possession; if they continued in their obstinate refusal, he would punish their leaders severely';

"and since, after that, Caecilius Simplex, member of the senate, approached for the same reason by the people of Gallilum who said that they would produce a tablet bearing on this matter from the emperor's archives, decided that 'it was courteous to give time for the production of proof' and allowed them the space of three months, to 1 December, on condition that, if a copy had not been produced by that date, he would act on the tablet which was in the province;

"So I, too, approached by the people of Gallilum who excused themselves for not yet having produced the copy and begged me to give them until 1 February next and to realise that this delay was to their advantage as occupiers, decree that the people of Gallilum must leave the territory of the people of Patulcum Campanum which they seized by force by 1 April next. If they do not obey this order, they must know that they will be liable to punishment for their long refusal to obey the law, which has now often been condemned."

In the council were: Marcus Julius Romulus, propraetorian legate, Titus Atilius Sabinus, propraetorian quaestor, *(and six others)*. Signatories: *(ten names follow)*.

The dispute was over the boundaries of two communities, fixed over a century and a half before by Marcus Metellus, consul in 115 BC. The inscriptions reveal both the persistence of a small community in asserting its claim, and the remarkable willingness of successive provincial governors over several years to allow a case to be reopened on apparently slender grounds. Sardinia became a senatorial province in 67, the senate losing Achaea when it was "freed" by Nero (cf. no. 46).

(c) VITELLIUS

52 **Denarius of Vitellius: Vitellius appeals to troop loyalty.**

Probably Dec. AD 68–Jan. 69

MW 38 = *BMC, Imp.* 1, p.306, no.65. *Mint in Upper Germany.*

Obverse: Clasped hands; FIDES EXERCITVVM = the loyalty of the armies.

Reverse: Clasped hands; FIDES PRAETORIANORVM = the loyalty of the Praetorians.

This coin was probably issued just before or after the proclamation of Vitellius as emperor on 1 January 69. The "armies" are in the first place those of Upper and Lower Germany; for the appeal to the praetorians to desert Galba, see Suetonius, *Galba* 16.

III. THE FLAVIANS

(a) VESPASIAN

53   Tampius and the Danube frontier.   Probably before AD 74

MW 274 = *ILS* 985. *Stone pedestal found at Fundi in Latium in* 1871.

> In honour of Lucius Tampius Flavianus, consul, proconsul of the province
> of Africa, imperial propraetorian legate of Pannonia, superintendent of the
> water supply ... awarded the decorations of a triumph ... [?for] receiving
> hostages from the tribes beyond the Danube, inspecting all their bound-
> aries and bringing the enemy over the river to pay taxes ... Lucius Tampius
> Rufus *(erected this)*.

The incident probably occurred during 69; the next year Tampius showed his
inability to control his own troops even though both he and they supported
Vespasian (Tacitus, *Histories* 3.10). His proconsulship of Africa was probably
in 70–71, and he gained a second consulship probably in 74. See no. 42 for
Transdanubians opposite Moesia shortly before this incident, and G. Townend,
JRS 51 (1961), 60.

54   Career of Dillius Vocula.   AD 70

MW 40 = *ILS* 983. *Copied at Rome once before ninth century (original now lost).*

> To Gaius Dillius Vocula, son of Aulus, of the tribe *Sergia*, military tribune
> of the first legion, member of the four-man commission for the roads,
> quaestor of the province of Pontus and Bithynia, plebeian tribune, praetor,
> legate of the twenty-second legion *Primigenia* in Germany. Helvia Procula,
> daughter of Titus, his wife, had this made.

Dillius Vocula played an important part in the campaign which eventually
suppressed the revolt of Civilis and Classicus in 70 (cf. Tacitus, *Histories*
4.24–59), taking over command of the troops of Upper Germany from the old
and incompetent Hordeonius Flaccus (4.25) and conducting operations doggedly
but without imagination (4.34). He was murdered in his camp at Novaesium
(Neuss) by a Roman deserter sent by Classicus, and his troops went over to the
rebels swearing allegiance to the "Empire of the Gauls" (4.59).

55   "Lex de imperio Vespasiani".   Probably January AD 70

MW 1 = *ILS* 244; *FIRA* 1.15. *Bronze tablet, fixed c.*1347 *to a wall of the church
of St. John Lateran by Cola di Rienzo; now in the Museo Capitolino.*

> ... and that he shall have the right to make ... or treaties[1] with whomso-
> ever he wishes, as was the right of deified Augustus, Tiberius Julius Caesar
> Augustus and Tiberius Claudius Caesar Augustus Germanicus:

---

[1] We do not know what Vespasian was empowered to make as well as treaties; perhaps 'peace' or 'war'.

And that he shall have the right to convene the senate, to put or refer proposals to the senate, to enact decrees of the senate by proposal and division of the house, as was the right of deified Augustus, Tiberius Julius Caesar Augustus, and Tiberius Claudius Caesar Augustus Germanicus:

And that when the senate meets by his wish, authority, order or command, or in his presence, the legality of all matters transacted shall be considered and established in the same way as if the meeting of the senate had been regularly summoned and held:

And that where he has 'commended'[1] a candidate for a magistracy, position of authority, command or any curatorship, or has granted or promised his vote, in any such election extraordinary consideration shall be given to such a candidate:

And that he shall have the right to extend and advance the boundary of the city of Rome[2] (whenever he considers it to be in the interest of the state), as was the right of Tiberius Claudius Caesar Augustus Germanicus:

And that whatsoever he deems to be of advantage to the state and its majesty in matters religious or secular, public or private, he shall have the right and power to act and perform, as was the case with deified Augustus, Tiberius Julius Caesar Augustus and Tiberius Claudius Caesar Augustus Germanicus:

And that if any law or plebiscite enacted that deified Augustus, Tiberius Julius Caesar Augustus or Tiberius Claudius Caesar Augustus Germanicus should not be bound by its terms, the emperor Caesar Vespasian is not to be bound by those laws or plebiscites, and that whatsoever rights of action were granted by any law or bill to deified Augustus, Tiberius Julius Caesar Augustus or Tiberius Claudius Caesar Augustus Germanicus shall all be granted to the emperor Caesar Vespasian Augustus:

And that all actions, decrees or commands effected by the emperor Caesar Vespasian Augustus or by anyone else at his order or command before the enactment of this law shall be as valid and binding as if they had been effected by order of the people or the *plebs*.

SANCTION

If anyone in consequence of this law has or shall have acted contrary to laws, bills, plebiscites or decrees of the senate, or if in consequence of this law he shall have failed to perform his obligations under any law, bill, plebiscite or decree of the senate, he is not to be held culpable on this account, nor is he on this account obliged to pay any public fine, nor may anyone institute against him on this account any legal action or judicial investigation, nor may anyone permit an action on this account to be brought before him in court.

This famous document, known as the *Lex de Imperio Vespasiani*, is a comprehensive grant of imperial power to the new emperor. This is the only extant document of its kind, and though it may be assumed that similar measures were

---

[1] A technical term for the emperor's nomination of individuals to elective magistracies and other offices.
[2] See next item.

enacted for later emperors, it is not safe to assume that the details of the grant
were identical in preceding reigns. The references to the rights of Augustus,
Tiberius and Claudius (note the omission of Gaius and Nero as well as the
brief reigns of Galba, Otho and Vitellius) may refer to *de facto* powers rather
than to legal rights. Although the document is a *lex*, the phrasing is similar to
that of a *senatus consultum*; this indicates the decline in importance of the
people.

The final clause conferring retrospective immunity was necessary because
Vespasian was proclaimed emperor at Alexandria on 1 July 69, months before
the Senate's decree, *c.* 20 December, and this law enacted in the popular assembly, early January 70.

The final clause of the "Sanction" refers to praetors or other magistrates
presiding over a court of law.

56   Vespasian extends the imperial boundaries and the boundary of Rome. AD 75

MW 51 = *NdS* (1933), p.241. *Travertine boundary marker, found* in situ *in Rome
near the corner of the Via della Torretta and the Via di Campo Marzio in 1930;
now in the Museo Nazionale.*

> The emperor Caesar Vespasian Augustus, *pontifex maximus*, holder of
> tribunician power six times, hailed as *Imperator* fourteen times, father of
> his country, censor, six times consul and designated for a seventh consul-
> ship, and Titus Caesar Vespasian, son of Augustus, hailed as *Imperator* six
> times, *pontifex*, holder of tribunician power four times, censor, four times
> consul and designated for a fifth consulship, extended the boundaries of
> the Roman empire and accordingly enlarged and defined the boundary of
> the city of Rome.
>
> *(on the left side)*   CLVIII

Marker of the boundary of the city of Rome *(pomerium)*, extended by
Vespasian in accordance with a provision of the *Lex de Imperio* (no. 55). Both
Claudius and Vespasian exercised the right while holding the (revived) traditional office of censor. Whatever the original rules governing the extension of
the *pomerium*, Claudius and Vespasian appear to have believed it was justified
by the extension of the imperial boundaries.

57   Vespasian preserves ritual and restores temples.   AD 78

MW 151 = *ILS* 252. *Stone seen by Poggio (fifteenth century) near the Capitol,
Rome.*

> To the emperor Caesar Vespasian Augustus, *pontifex maximus*, holder of
> tribunician power [nine times], hailed as *Imperator* seventeen times, eight
> times consul and designated for a ninth consulship, censor, who preserved
> the public ceremonies and restored the sacred temples: erected by the
> Brotherhood of Titius.

The *Sodales Titii* were a very ancient order of priests revived like the Arval
Brotherhood (cf. no. 69) by Augustus, connected by Romans with the Sabine
king Titus Tatius (cf. Tacitus, *Annals* 1.54), but whose origins and functions

remain obscure. (The "Trib. Pot." number is restored to fit the consular years, but the "Imp." number is inconsistent with them – Vespasian was "Imp. XVIII" by 2 December 76.)

58   Career of Eprius Marcellus.   After AD 74

MW 271 = *ILS* 992. *Found near Capua; now in Naples Museum.*

> In honour of Titus Clodius Eprius Marcellus, son of Marcus, of the tribe *Falerna*, consul twice, augur, chief priest of the Curiae, priest of Augustus, *praetor peregrinus*, and proconsul of Asia for three years, the province of Cyprus *(erected this).*

The famous *delator* (accuser) of Thrasea Paetus under Nero, Eprius Marcellus was made *praetor peregrinus* by Claudius in 48 for one day to fill a vacancy; he was consul first under Nero in 66 and for the second time under Vespasian in 74; he was proconsul of Asia probably from 70 to 73. He committed suicide in 79 after conspiring with Caecina against Vespasian. Cf. Tacitus, *Annals* 12.4; 16.22ff; *Histories* 4.6ff.

59   Sohaemus, king of Emesa.

MW 239 = *ILS* 8958. *Baalbek (Heliopolis), Syria.*

> In honour of His Majesty King Gaius Julius Sohaemus, son of His Majesty King Samsigeramus, friend of Caesar and the Romans, awarded the insignia of a consul … patron of the colony, duovir for five years, Lucius Vitellius Sossianus, son of Lucius, of the tribe *Fabia, (erected this).*

Sohaemus was king of Emesa on the Syrian border from 54. It was probably a relation, also called Sohaemus, who was made client king of Sophene on the upper Euphrates about the same time. Julius Sohaemus probably relinquished his throne with full honours soon after 72. The colony at Heliopolis had been founded by Agrippa in the time of Augustus. Note the king's Roman citizenship and distinctions. For other patrons see no. 19 *note.*

60   The Flavians and Mithridates, king of Iberia.   AD 75

MW 237 = *ILS* 8795; *IGRR* 3.133; *OGIS* 1.379. *Stone found at Mcheta (Harmozica, Armenia Major) in* 1867; *now in Tiflis Museum.*

> The emperor Caesar Vespasian Augustus, *pontifex maximus*, in the seventh year of his tribunician power, hailed as *Imperator* fourteen times, consul for the sixth time and designated for a seventh term, father of his country, censor, and the emperor Titus Caesar, son of Augustus, in the fifth year of his tribunician power, consul for the fourth time and designated for a fifth term, censor, and Domitian Caesar, son of Augustus, consul for the third time and designated for a fourth term, fortified these walls for Mithridates, son of king Pharasmanes, king of the Iberians, and for Iamaspus[1] his son, friend of Caesar and the Roman people, and for the tribe of the Iberians.

---

[1] Or Iamasdes or Iamasaspus.

Pharasmanes appears in Tacitus, *Annals* 12.44–51; 13.37; Mithridates succeeded his father in 75. The Caucasian kingdom of Iberia was a somewhat tenuous client of Rome. After the restoration of harmony between Rome and Parthia by Nero (see no. 44), Vologaeses of Parthia felt able to ask for a joint defence against raids by the Alani from north of the Caucasus. Vespasian rejected this, but the inscription shows that he took his own measures notwithstanding. Cf. Suetonius, *Domitian*, 2; Dio 65.15.3.

61   Berenice and Agrippa II.

MW 244 = *Mélanges de l'Univ. St. Jos. Beyrouth*, 25 (1942–3), p.32. *Limestone found c.1926 near the Grand Mosque in Beirut; now in the National Museum at Beirut.*

> Queen Berenice, daughter of His Majesty King Agrippa, and King Agrippa restored completely this (?temple) built by King Herod their great-grandfather which had fallen down through age and adorned it with marble *(pavements or statues)* and six columns.

Berenice, born in 18, was daughter of Agrippa I of Judaea; after the death of her husband in 48 she lived with her brother Agrippa II (cf. *Acts of the Apostles* 25, 13ff.) Titus fell in love with her when in Judaea (67–70), and she visited Rome in 75 and 79. Her great-grandfather was Herod the Great.

(b) TITUS

62   Pactumeius, first consul from Africa.   After AD 79

MW 298 = *ILA* 2.644. *Marble from Cirta in North Africa.*

> In honour of Quintus Aurelius Pactumeius Fronto, son of Publius, of the tribe *Quirina*, enrolled among the praetorians in the senate by the emperor Caesar Vespasian Augustus and the emperor Titus, son of Augustus, member of the Fetial priesthood, prefect of the *aerarium militare*, the first consul to come from Africa, Pactumeia ... erected this as a gift for the best of fathers.

Pactumeius was consul in 80. Spain and Gallia Narbonensis had already produced consuls, but Africa later outstripped them. Cirta was the old Numidian capital, where Julius Caesar had settled a number of Italians, among them probably the ancestors of Pactumeius. The mention of his being the first consul from Africa indicates the natural pride of the provincials in their gradual advance to high office.

63   Restoration of the *Aqua Claudia*.   (a) AD 71; (b) 81

MW 408 = *ILS* 218. *Two of three inscriptions on the Porta Maggiore in Rome.*

> (a) The emperor Caesar Vespasian Augustus, *pontifex maximus*, in the second year of his tribunician power, hailed as *Imperator* six times, consul for the third time and designated for a fourth term, father of his country,

restored at his own expense for the benefit of the city the Curtian and Caerulean aqueducts which had been built by deified Claudius but had been neglected for nine years and allowed to fall into disrepair.

(b) The emperor Titus Caesar Vespasian Augustus, son of deified Vespasian, *pontifex maximus*, in the tenth year of his tribunician power, hailed as *Imperator* seventeen times, father of his country, censor, and in his eighth consulship, arranged that the Curtian and Caerulean aqueducts, originally built by deified Claudius and later repaired for the benefit of the city by his own father deified Vespasian, should be rebuilt from the ground up at his own expense to a new design as they had collapsed from their source through age.

These aqueducts, usually known as the *Aqua Claudia*, were built by Claudius in 52. They stretch for 69 kilometres from Subiaco to the Caelian Hill; only the last 14.5 kilometres were carried on arches. The Porta Maggiore was built to carry them as they enter Rome and was later incorporated in the Aurelian walls.

64   Flavian road-building in Asia Minor.   AD 80

MW 105 = *ILS* 263. *Marble milestone on the road between Ancyra and Dorylaeum, recorded by Hamilton in the eighteenth century.*

The emperor Titus Caesar Augustus, son of deified Vespasian, *pontifex maximus*, holder of tribunician power ten times, hailed as *Imperator* fifteen times, eight times consul, censor, father of his country, and Caesar (Domitian, son of the deified), seven times consul, leader of the Roman youth, through the agency of Aulus Caesennius Gallus, propraetorian legate, built the roads of the provinces of Galatia, Cappadocia, Pontus, Pisidia, Paphlagonia, Lycaonia and Lesser Armenia. LXXI.

The words in brackets were erased after Domitian's death as part of his official condemnation *(damnatio memoriae)*. Caesennius Gallus commanded the legion XII *Fulminata*, which reduced Galilee in 66, reached the consulship under Vespasian, governed a province made up of the seven districts named, and was still in office in 82. The Flavians undertook an extensive programme of road-building in Asia Minor.

65   Titus destroys Jerusalem.   AD 80

MW 53 = *ILS* 264. *From an arch at Rome in the Circus Maximus, copied once before the ninth century; now lost.*

The senate and people of Rome *(dedicated this)* to the emperor Titus Caesar Vespasian Augustus, son of deified Vespasian, *pontifex maximus*, holder of tribunician power ten times, hailed as *Imperator* seventeen times, eight times consul, father of his country, their *princeps*, because following his father's instructions and advice, and under his auspices, he subdued the people of the Jews and destroyed the city of Jerusalem which before him generals, kings and peoples all assaulted in vain or left entirely untouched.

This inscription comes from an arch no longer surviving. The Arch of Titus (no. 66) has well-known relief sculptures of the spoils from the Temple in Jerusalem, including the table of shewbread, trumpets and seven-branched candlestick (photo in Donald E. Strong, *The Classical World*, no.65). The claim made in the last clause is a manifest exaggeration: apart from non-Romans, Pompey had entered the city and the Temple.

66   Dedication of the Arch of Titus, Rome.   After AD 81

MW 108 = *ILS 265. Still* in situ.

The senate and people of Rome to deified Titus Vespasian Augustus, son of deified Vespasian.

Cf. no. 65.

(c) DOMITIAN

67   The constitution of Salpensa.   AD 81–84

MW 453 = *ILS 6088; FIRA 1.23. Bronze tablet; two columns of writing. Found with no. 68 near Málaga in 1851; now in Madrid.*

XXI: Title: Magistrates to obtain Roman citizenship

... Any man who is appointed duovir, aedile or quaestor in accordance with this constitution shall become a Roman citizen at the end of his year of office, together with his parents and wife and any children born of a legal marriage and still under the authority of their father, also with any grandsons and granddaughters on the male side who are under their father's authority; on condition that the number of those who become Roman citizens shall not exceed the number of those allowed to become magistrates under the terms of this constitution.

XXII: Title: Those who are given Roman citizenship remain under the legal dominion, marital control, or parental power of the same people as before

Any man or woman who has been given Roman citizenship under this constitution or by any edict of the emperor Caesar Augustus Vespasian or of the emperor Titus Caesar Augustus or of the emperor Caesar Augustus Domitian, father of his country, shall remain under the authority of the man who has been made a Roman citizen by this constitution, whether as children, wife or dependants, just as would have been the case if the change to Roman citizenship had not taken place, and they shall have the same right of choosing a guardian as they would have had if they had been born the sons or daughters of a Roman citizen instead of becoming so later.

XXIII: Title: Those who are given Roman citizenship retain their rights over their freedmen

Any man or woman who has been granted Roman citizenship under this constitution or by an edict of the emperor Caesar Vespasian Augustus or of the emperor Titus Caesar Vespasian Augustus or of the emperor Caesar

Domitian Augustus shall retain the same rights and control over all freedmen and freedwomen, whether his own or his father's assuming they have not acquired Roman citizenship themselves, and over their possessions and over the services undertaken by them in exchange for their freedom, as they would have had if their change of citizenship had not taken place.

(Paragraphs XXIIII and XXV are about the powers and privileges of temporary officials with the title of prefect)

XXVI: Title: On the oath to be sworn by duovirs, aediles and quaestors

All the present duovirs with judicial power, all aediles and all quaestors of this *municipium* shall each during the five days following the publication of this constitution swear an oath publicly in the name of Jupiter and deified Augustus, deified Claudius, deified Vespasian Augustus and deified Titus Augustus and the genius of the emperor Caesar Domitian Augustus and by the *(municipal)* guardian gods, that they shall duly perform whatever they consider is in accordance with this constitution and in the common interest of the townspeople of the *municipium* of Flavia Salpensa, and shall not knowingly perform out of malice or deceit anything contrary to this constitution or to the common interest of the townspeople, and shall prevent anyone else they can from doing so; and they shall not allow any meeting of the decurions to be held and shall not give or publish any opinion except as they consider to be in accordance with this constitution and the common interest of the *municipium*. The same oath shall be sworn by all those who subsequently become duovir, aedile or quaestor within five days of assuming office and before the decurions or *conscripti* meet. Anyone who fails to swear this oath shall pay a fine of 10,000 sesterces to the townspeople of the *municipium*, and any townsman of the *municipium* who so chooses and is granted the right by this constitution may bring a charge, suit or prosecution against him for this sum.

(Paragraphs XXVII–XXIX are about the magistrates' veto, the freeing of slaves and the appointing of guardians).

Paragraphs XXI–XXIX survive on one bronze tablet from the code of laws for the *municipium* of Salpensa, a town in Hispania Baetica not certainly identified. The inscription was found at Málaga in the same province, which suggests that it was made there and was never actually erected; the fact that Domitian's name has not been deleted supports this theory.

The last clause of XXI was added to prevent magistrates' retiring during their year of office to allow others to replace them and thus obtain citizenship.

Vespasian granted Latin rights to all the communities in Spain (Pliny, *Natural History* 3.30), and the process of granting constitutions to them (Salpensa and Malaca being only two out of some four hundred) obviously took many years. Modelled on Italian institutions, they show the stress on local autonomy and the access to full Roman citizenship of the local notables through the holding of public office. See next item for a similar constitution from Málaga.

68   The constitution of Malaca.   AD 81–84

MW 454 = *ILS* 6089; *FIRA* 1.24. *Bronze tablet; five columns of writing. Found with no. 67 near Málaga in 1851; now in Madrid.*

LI: Title: Rules for nomination of candidates

If by nomination day no candidates or fewer than the required number have been nominated, or if of the candidates nominated fewer than the required number are eligible for office, then the returning officer[1] shall post in a place where it can be clearly read from ground level a list of names of persons eligible for office by the terms of this constitution to make up the number required for office under this constitution. Those so posted may if they like go to the returning officer and each name an additional person of the same status; these also may if they wish in the same manner and before the same returning officer nominate each one extra person; the returning officer shall then post the names of all these candidates in a place where they can be clearly read from ground level, and he shall then hold the elections with them all as candidates, exactly as if they had all been properly nominated by the right day according to the section of this constitution on standing for office and had stood voluntarily and had not originally withheld their candidacy.[2]

(Paragraphs LII and LIII are about how the elections are to be conducted)

LIIII: Title: Which candidates are eligible for office

The returning officer shall first see to the election of duovirs with judicial powers from the category of free-born persons carefully prescribed by this constitution; next he shall see to the election of aediles and then quaestors from the category of free-born persons carefully prescribed by this constitution; he shall not allow anyone to stand for the duovirate who is under twenty-five or has held the office in the previous five years, and no one for the aedileship or quaestorship who is under twenty-five or is subject to any restriction which would bar him from becoming one of the decurions or *conscripti* if he were a Roman citizen.

LV: Title: Voting procedure

The returning officer shall call the townspeople to vote by *curiae*[3] in such a way that all the *curiae* shall be called to vote at the same time, and each shall go into its individual enclosure and vote by tablets. He shall also appoint three of the townspeople of the *municipium* to look after the ballot-box of each of the *curiae*; they must not belong to that *curia*, and their job is to guard the votes and count them; and he must arrange that first each of them swears to carry out the count and report the result honestly. And he should allow the candidates also to station one inspector at each of the

---

[1] The senior duovir would normally act as returning officer.
[2] This section is often taken to be evidence of a growing unwillingness to hold civic office, but in fact is just designed to cover every contingency: see the later sections for a similar approach.
[3] The *curiae* were "wards" or "constituencies".

ballot-boxes. The inspectors appointed by the returning officer and by the candidates shall all vote in the *curia* where they are on duty, and their vote shall be just as legal and valid as if they had voted in their own *curia*.

LVI: Title: What to do if there is a tie

The returning officer shall declare the candidate receiving most votes from any one *curia* duly elected and appointed for that *curia*, until the required number of officers has been supplied. If in any *curia* two or more candidates score the same number of votes, then he shall give a married man or one with the rights of a married man precedence over an unmarried man without children and without the rights of a married man, one with children precedence over one without, and one with more children precedence over one with fewer, and shall declare him elected; two children lost after the naming ceremony, or one boy after puberty or girl of marriageable age lost shall count as one living child.[1] If two or more candidates have the same number of votes and are of the same standing, he shall resort to lots and declare the one whose name is drawn out first elected by lot.

(Paragraphs LVII–LX deal with the declaration of the results and oaths to be taken by the successful candidates)

(Paragraph LXI deals with the adoption of a patron for the municipium)

LXII: Title: Destruction of buildings (except for reconstruction) prohibited

No one may unroof, destroy or arrange for the demolition of any building in the town of the *municipium* of Flavia Malaca or in the suburbs thereof without the approval of the decurions or *conscripti* (there being at least half the members present), unless he intends to rebuild it within a year. Anyone who breaks this law shall pay as a fine the value of the building to the townspeople of the *municipium* of Flavia Malaca, and any townsman of the *municipium* who so chooses and is granted the right by this constitution may bring a charge, suit or prosecution against him for this sum.

(Paragraphs LXIII–LXIX are about various legal and financial arrangements, such as fines, contracts, public funds)

Paragraphs LI–LXIX on one bronze tablet from the code of laws for the *municipium* of Malaca in Hispania Baetica; it is less carelessly inscribed than the Salpensa code (see previous item) and is in another hand. This one seems to have been erected, for the name of Domitian has been deleted (paragraph LIX) in the normal way. The fragments supplement each other. Note in the Málaga code the detailed provisions for fair elections.

69   A conspiracy against Domitian.   AD 87

MW 14 Col. 2 lines 62–65. *Marble Tablet, found 1867–70 in the excavations of the sacred grove of the Arval Brotherhood (the Vigna Ceccarelli) near Rome: now in the Museo Nazionale, Rome.*

[1] The privileges for those with children follow Augustus' *Lex Papia-Poppaea.*

From the ACTS OF THE ARVAL BROTHERS

In the same consulship *(sc. Gaius Cilnius Proculus and Lucius Neratius Priscus, coss. suff. 87)* on 22 September on the Capitol because of the detection of the crimes of wicked men, in the mastership of Gaius Julius Silanus, Gaius Venuleius Apronianus sacrificed on the Capitol one ox.

No details of this conspiracy are known, but it appears to mark the beginning of Domitian's unpopularity; perhaps a defeat at the hands of the Dacians in 86 and the recall of Agricola in 84 or 85 had something to do with it. It was followed on 1 January 89 by the more serious revolt of Antonius Saturninus, governor of Upper Germany.

The Arval Brotherhood was an ancient priestly college, revived under Augustus, whose traditional rites honoured Dea Dia but now also honoured the Imperial House. Their members were drawn from the high aristocracy, and they elected an annual "master" *(magister)*. Cf. no. 49.

70   An equestrian career under the Flavians.

MW 372 = *ILS* 9200. *Stone found at Baalbek (Heliopolis), Syria.*

For Gaius Velius Rufus, son of Salvius, chief centurion of the twelfth legion *Fulminata*, commander of detachments of nine legions – the first and second *Adiutrix*, the second and eighth *Augusta*, the ninth *Hispana*, the fourteenth *Gemina*, the twentieth *Victrix*, the twenty-first *Rapax*,[1] tribune of the thirteenth Urban cohort, commander of the African and Mauretanian army for subduing the tribes in Mauretania,[2] presented in the Judaean War[3] by the emperor Vespasian and the emperor Titus the crown for ramparts[4] and with collars, medals and armlets, also presented with the crown for sieges and with two silver spearheads and two silver-mounted banners, and presented in the war against the Marcomanni, Quadi and Sarmatae[5] with a crown for sieges, two silver spearheads and two silver-mounted banners for making an expedition against the Sarmatae through the territory of Decebalus, king of the Dacians[6]; procurator of the emperor Caesar Augustus Germanicus *(i.e. Domitian)* of the province of Pannonia and Dalmatia, procurator of Rhaetia with power of life and death. He was sent to Parthia and brought back Epiphanes and Callinicus, sons of king Antiochus,[7] to the emperor Vespasian together with a vast band of his

---

[1] This force of legionary detachments was employed in the war against the Chatti, 83–84; only eight of the nine legions are mentioned, and the missing name should probably be that of the eleventh *Claudia* which was also serving in Germany.

[2] Probably 84–85.

[3] 66–70, when Rufus will have been a legionary centurion.

[4] The *corona vallaris*, originally presented to the first man to cross the enemy rampart, and the *corona muralis*, originally presented to the first man to scale the enemy walls, were awards for bravery normally reserved for centurions and above. Collars, medals and armlets *(torques, phalerae, armillae)* were awarded to all ranks up to centurion. The silver spearhead *(hasta pura)* was presented to senior centurions and above. The *vexillum*, a silver-mounted banner, was also only presented to senior officers.

[5] 89, ostensibly because they had not helped Rome against Dacia.

[6] Decebalus defeated a Roman army in 86 but was defeated in 88, after which peace was made in 89.

[7] Antiochus IV of Commagene was deposed in 72; Epiphanes and Callinicus, his sons, put up some resistance but were forced to flee to Parthia where king Vologeses entertained them till Velius Rufus demanded their surrender to Vespasian.

subjects. Marcus Alfius Olympiacus, son of Marcus, of the tribe *Fabia*, standard-bearer and veteran of the fifteenth legion *Apollinaris* put this up in his honour.

A remarkably active and successful military career. As often, his earlier centurionates are omitted.

71   A centurion of Domitian in Dacia and Germany.   Probably before AD 96

MW 58 = *ILS* 2127. *Tombstone with crown above the inscription and cavalryman with spear below, found at Carthage, now in Algiers Museum.*

> Dedicated to the spirits of the departed: Quintus Vilanius Nepos, son of Quintus, of the tribe *Voltinia*, citizen of Philippi, centurion of the thirteenth urban cohort, decorated by Domitian for *(services in)* the Dacian war, also by Domitian for *(services in)* the German war, also awarded *(silver)* collars and bracelets for *(services in)* the Dacian war; he lived for fifty years, served in the army for thirty-two: Marcus Silius Quintianus, *optio*, set this up to his benefactor.

The thirteenth urban cohort was at this time stationed at Carthage. Later it moved to Lyons. Exceptionally for an urban cohort, it may have taken part in active operations under Domitian. The German war probably refers to Domitian's operations against the Chatti in 89, for which he celebrated a triumph. Vilanius was decorated twice in the Dacian war of 88–89, once in the German. *Optio* was the rank next below centurion.

72   A Competitor in Domitian's Capitoline Games.   During or after AD 94

MW 64 = *ILS* 5177; *IGRR* 1.350–2; Gordon 153; *IG* 14.2012. *Gravestone found at Rome not far from the Colline Gate in 1871; now in the Museo Capitolino.*

(below the portrait)

> Dedicated to the spirits of the departed: Quintus Sulpicius Maximus, son of Quintus, of the tribe *Claudia*, from Rome, lived eleven years five months and twelve days. On the third *lustrum* of the *(Capitoline)* games he appeared in competition with fifty-two Greek poets and his genius changed the applause won by his tender years to admiration, and he finished the competition with distinction. Extemporary verses were submitted to him so that his parents should not appear to have been unduly influenced by their natural feelings. Quintus Sulpicius Eugramus and Licinia Januaria, his unfortunate parents, set this up in memory of their devoted son for themselves and their descendants.

This large monument surmounted by a gable crowned with a wreath has a bas-relief portrait of Sulpicius holding a scroll in his left hand. To the left and right of the portrait is a poem in Greek hexameters over thirty lines long preceded by "Impromptu poem of Quintus Sulpicius Maximus: what words would Zeus have used when chiding Helios for giving his chariot to Phaethon?" (The poem's conclusion is on the scroll in the portrait). The Latin inscription follows below, and below again are two short Greek epitaphs on Sulpicius in elegiac couplets.

In 86 Domitian instituted games in honour of Capitoline Jupiter. They were to be repeated at four-yearly intervals and were on the Greek model (cf. no. 39), including contests in literature as well as athletics. See Suetonius, *Domitian* 4. The third *lustrum* (occasion) was in 94. Sulpicius' father's *cognomen* indicates that he was a freedman. Sulpicius does not seem to have won a prize, nor does his poem suggest that, for all his youth, he should have won one.

73   Assassination of Domitian.   AD 96

SN 15. *Consular list* (Fasti Ostienses), *Ostia.*

	C. Manlius Valens
	C. Antistius Vetus
1 May	Q. Fabius Postuminus
	T. Prifernius [Paetus?]
1 Sept.	Ti. Caesius Fronto
	M. Calpurnius ... icus
18 Sept.	Domitian was killed. On the same day Marcus Cocceius Nerva was proclaimed Emperor. 19 Sept., [it was ratified by] a decree of the senate ...

For accession of Nerva, see also next item and SN 148d = *YCS* 7 (1940).

IV. NERVA AND TRAJAN

(a) NERVA

74   "Liberty" restored by Nerva.   AD 96

MW 66 = SN 27a = *ILS* 274. *Copied once before the ninth century from a monument then on the Capitolium at Rome; now lost.*

> To LIBERTY restored by the emperor Nerva Caesar Augustus in the eight hundred and forty-eighth year from the foundation of Rome on the eighteenth of September: the senate and people of Rome.

The day of Domitian's assassination (see previous item) was acclaimed by the Senate at least as the day when Liberty was restored to the state; cf. Pliny, *Letters* 9.13.4 and Tacitus, *Agricola* 3. The claim to be the restorer of liberty was, however, conventional – it was made by Augustus e.g. in *Res Gestae* 1. See also next item.

75   Aureus of Nerva. Nerva "restores Liberty".   AD 96

SN 27b = *BMC, Imp.* 3, p.3, no.16. *Mint of Rome.*

> *Obverse:* Laureate head of Nerva; around, IMP. NERVA CAES. AVG. P.M.TR.P.COS.II P.P.

> *Reverse:* Libertas, holding *pileus* (cap of freedom) and sceptre; around, LIBERTAS PVBLICA = the freedom of the *(Roman)* people.

The reverse type alludes to the end of the tyranny of Domitian (see previous item).

76   Coins of Nerva: the official viewpoint (a), (b) AD 96; (c), (d), (e) 97; (f) 98

SN 91. *Mint of Rome.* (a), (d) aurei; (b), (e) denarii; (c) sestertius; (f) silver quinarius.

(a) *Aureus*, 96. *BMC, Imp.* 3, p.1, no.4.

> *Obverse:* Laureate head of Nerva; around, IMP. NERVA CAES. AVG. P.M. TR.P. COS.II P.P.

> *Reverse:* Clasped hands; CONCORDIA EXERCITVVM = the concord of the armies.

The reverse type alludes, hopefully, to the factor on which Nerva's survival as emperor depended.

(b) Denarius, 96. *BMC, Imp.* 3, p.4, no.22.

> *Obverse:* Laureate head of Nerva; around, IMP. NERVA CAES. AVG. PONT.MAX. TR.P.

> *Reverse:* Diana; COS.II DESIGN.III P.P.

(c) Sestertius, 97. *BMC, Imp.* 3, p.21, no.118.

> *Obverse:* Laureate head of Nerva; around, IMP. NERVA CAES. AVG. P.M. TR.P. COS.III P.P.

> *Reverse:* Rome seated, holding a Victory and a spear; ROMA RENASCENS = Rome reborn, S.C.

The theme of "Rome reborn" was on the coinage of Galba, Vitellius and Vespasian; its propagandist tone is obvious.

(d) Aureus, 97. *BMC, Imp.* 3, p.8, no.59.

> *Obverse:* Laureate head of Nerva; around, IMP. NERVA CAES. AVG. P.M. TR.P.II COS.III P.P.

> *Reverse:* Justice seated, holding a sceptre and a branch; IVSTITIA AVGVST.

Iustitia – Justice – was a cardinal imperial virtue, though not common on coins. Here it doubtless refers to Nerva's distinction as a lawyer.

(e) Denarius, 97. *BMC, Imp.* 3, p.9, no.63.

> *Obverse:* Laureate head of Nerva; around, IMP. NERVA CAES. AVG. GERM. P.M. TR.P.II

> *Reverse:* Liberty holding a *pileus* (cap of freedom) and a sceptre; IMP.II COS.III DESIGN.IIII P.P.

Dated to the end of 97. The title Germanicus refers to Trajan's success in Upper Germany. The image of Liberty repeats the anti-tyrannical theme so prominent under Nerva (cf. nos. 74–5).

(f) Silver quinarius, 98. *BMC, Imp.* 3, p.10, no.68.

> *Obverse:* Laureate head of Nerva; around, IMP. NERVA CAES. AVG. GERM. P.M. TR.P.II.

> *Reverse:* Victory holding a wreath and a palm; IMP.II COS.IIII P.P.

Early 98. A typical victory coin, without a legend. Even pacific emperors had to have, or claim, military success.

77   Sestertius of Nerva: Nerva and the Corn-Supply.   AD 97

SN 29 = *BMC, Imp.* 3, p.21, no.115. *Mint of Rome.*

> *Obverse:* Laureate head of Nerva; around, IMP. NERVA CAES. AVG. P.M.TR.P.COS.III P.P.

> *Reverse: Modius* (corn-measure); on either side, S C; around, PLEBEI VRBANAE FRVMENTO CONSTITVTO = *(in record of)* the organisation of the corn-supply for the people of Rome.

The maintenance of the corn-supply for the people of Rome was one of the first duties of a Roman emperor; the precarious position of Nerva demanded that propaganda gestures be made to every section of the community.

78 Sestertius of Nerva: Nerva and the imperial postal service. AD 97

SN 30 = *BMC, Imp.* 3, p.21, no.119. *Mint of Rome.*

Obverse: Laureate head of Nerva; around, IMP. NERVA CAES. AVG. P.M.TR.P.COS.III P.P.

Reverse: Two mules grazing in front of tipped-up cart; on either side, S C; around, VEHICVLATIONE ITALIAE REMISSA = *(in record of)* the relieving of Italy from the duty of providing animals for the Imperial postal service.

The maintenance of the *cursus publicus* was a heavy burden on the local communities. Claudius had tried in vain to prevent abuses (SG 375 = *ILS* 214). Nerva transferred the task in Italy to the central government, but in the provinces it remained a local responsibility.

(b) TRAJAN

79 Building at Caerleon. AD 99 or 100

SN 314 = *RIB* 330. *Marble commemorative slab found at Caerleon (Isca) in 1928.*

For the emperor Caesar Nerva Trajan Augustus Germanicus, son of deified Nerva, *pontifex maximus*, holder of tribunician power, father of his country, three[1] times consul, the second legion *Augusta (built this)*.

The slab had been reused on the site of a stone exercise hall, the original building of which it may commemorate. The natural result of the achievement of stable frontiers was the construction of stone-built forts and buildings for the permanent garrisons (see LACTOR 4 no. 29 (28)).

80 The *alimenta* system. AD 101

SN 435 = *CIL* 9.1455; *ILS* 6509; *FIRA* 3.117. *Near Beneventum.*

In the fourth consulship of the emperor Caesar Nerva Trajan Augustus Germanicus, and that of Quintus Articuleius Paetus, in accordance with the instructions of the best and greatest emperor, those whose names are written below have mortgaged properties so that from the loan the Baebian Ligurians may receive the interest written below every six months and out of his kindness boys and girls may receive support.

(The terms of 66 mortgages are then set out of which the following are examples)

By Crispia Restituta: The Pomponian farms, in the Beneventan territory, in the Aequan district, in the Ligurian area, beside Nasidius Vitalis, valued at 50,000 sesterces, a loan of 3,520 sesterces. Interest 88 sesterces.

By Lucius Naeratius Diadumenus: the Rubrian farms in the Beneventan territory, Ligurian district, valued at 34,000 sesterces for a loan of 1,000 sesterces. Interest 25 sesterces.

[1] Originally written "two" and changed, presumably in the interval between drafting and completion.

By Titus Amunius Silvanus: the Trebellian and Appian farms with
(circeis?) in the Roman district valued at 46,000 sesterces for a loan of
4,000 sesterces. Interest 100 sesterces.

By Neratius Corellius: the Paccian farms and the Aurelian cottages next
to Julius Saturninus valued at 22,000 sesterces, for a loan of 2,000 sesterces. Neratius Marcellus pays in interest 50 sesterces.

By Gnaeus Marcius Rufinus: the Marcian and Satrian farms valued at
130,000 sesterces, also the Julian farms valued at 14,000 sesterces, also the
Avillian farms valued at 42,000 sesterces, also the Vitellian and Nasenian
and Marcellian farms next to Suellius Flaccus valued at 120,000 sesterces
for a loan of 10,000 sesterces; also the Curian and Satrian farms in the
Herculanean district next to Tettius Etruscus valued at 35,000[1] sesterces
for a loan of 3,000 sesterces; also the Albian farms with cottages in the
Meflan district next to Nonius Restitutus valued at 110,000 sesterces for a
loan of 10,000 sesterces, also mortgaged for the ninth time the Caesian
farms in the Beneventan territory, Tucian district, next to Messius Aper
valued at 50,000 sesterces for a loan of 3,000 sesterces. Total 466,000 sesterces for a loan of 42,440 sesterces. Interest 1,061 sesterces.
(The remaining entries are similar).

The *alimenta* system aimed at providing money for the upbringing of the children of needy parents and Italian family to maintain the Italian stock; its greatest
expansion was under Trajan. The emperor lent money to farmers (on a small
enough part of the value of the farm to ensure viability: it is around 12% here
though it varies): interest at 5% was paid on this into a special fund set aside
to provide support for a fixed number of children decided beforehand (the low
interest rate also ensured payment). Although the rate of interest was low, it
constituted a permanent charge on the estate and hence was not necessarily
advantageous to the owner.

The definitive study is by Duncan-Jones, *Papers of the British School at Rome*,
32 (1964), 123–146.

Cf. nos. 81 and 96.

81   Pomponius Bassus administers the *alimenta*.   19 October AD 101 or 102

SN 437 = *ILS* 6106. *Rome.*

During the consulship of Lucius Arruntius Stella and Lucius Julius
Marinus on 19 October, Manius Acilius Placidus and Lucius Petronius
Fronto, being two of the four chief magistrates, consulted the senate of
Ferentinum meeting in the court-house of the temple of Mercury. As
recorders there were present Quintus Segiarnus Maecianus and Titus
Munnius Nomantinus.

Whereas all agreed that Titus Pomponius Bassus, the distinguished
senator, in accordance with the emperor's generosity, was performing so
well the administrative duty entrusted to him by our most generous
emperor Caesar Nerva Trajan Augustus Germanicus, that is the duty

---

[1] This sum is omitted in the final total.

through which Trajan has secured for ever the future of his Italy, that the whole age ought to be deservedly thankful for his administration; and again that a man of such excellence would be a great help to this town: in this matter the following was decreed in accordance with what it seemed should be done.

"This House agrees that representatives from among its members be sent to Titus Pomponius Bassus, the distinguished senator, to present the request that he deign to receive this town as a client of his flourishing house, and that he permit himself to be appointed patron once a tablet inscribed with this decree is placed in his house."

The motion was passed.

The representatives who carried out the task were Aulus Caecilius Quirinalis, son of Aulus, and Quirinalis' son.

Pomponius Bassus was consul in 94, governor of Cappadocia 95–100, and then in charge of the administration of the *alimenta* (see previous item).

The emperors permitted the relationship of patron to client community to continue; it now had no direct political significance. The patron was honoured by the choice, and the client expected (as boldly stated here) the influence of their patron to be of benefit to them. Cf. no. 19 *note*.

82   The equestrian career of Titinius Capito.

MW 347 = *ILS* 1448. *Marble found in Rome; now in the Capitoline Museum.*

Gnaeus Octavius Titinius Capito, commander of a cohort, military tribune, awarded a silver spearhead and a crown for ramparts, in charge of the correspondence and imperial property *(of Domitian – name tactfully suppressed)*, then in charge of the correspondence of deified Nerva and at his suggestion awarded the insignia of a praetor by decree of the senate, then in charge of correspondence for a third time to the emperor Nerva Caesar Trajan Augustus Germanicus, and commander of the Watch, made this offering to Vulcan.

A highly successful equestrian career under Domitian, Nerva and Trajan. Pliny the Younger writes of Titinius Capito's services to literature in *Letters* 1.17 and 8.12. He was in charge of the correspondence of the three emperors without a break. By the end of the first century, the imperial secretaryships were held by *Equites* and not freedmen as under Claudius.

83   Equestrian career of Vibius Salutaris.   AD 104

SN 493a = *ILS* 7193. *From the theatre at Ephesus.*

In honour of Diana of Ephesus and the Ephesian council Gaius Vibius Salutaris, son of Gaius, of the tribe *Oufentina*, manager of harbour-dues for the province of Sicily, manager in charge of purchasing the corn supply, prefect of the cohort of Astures and Callaeci, military tribune of the loyal and faithful twenty-second legion *Primigenia*, assistant governor of the province of Mauretania Tingitana and also of the province of Belgica, put up at his own expense a silver statue of Diana and also two silver statuettes, one representing the city of Rome, and the other the council *(of Ephesus)*, so that during each assembly they might be put on their pedestals; for the dedication of these he entrusted for allocation by the council 17,000 sesterces.

A Greek version follows with minor variations, ending:

... put up from his private resources a silver statue of Artemis and two silver statuettes, one of Rome the chief city of the empire, and the other of the council faithful to the emperor, which he consecrated so that they may be put on their pedestals during an assembly, as his instructions laid down. And he consecrated also for allocation by the council 4,250 denarii. *(This was)* during the proconsulship of Gaius Aquilius Proculus, when the post of Town Clerk *(Grammateus)* was held for the second time by Tiberius Claudius Julianus faithful to his emperor and country.

An equestrian career of late Flavian date. See A. N. Sherwin-White, *Roman Society and Roman Law in the New Testament*, 90, for the question of the silver statues of Diana and possible connection with Paul's experience at Ephesus (*Acts* 19.23ff.).

84   Denarius of Trajan: Trajan, "best of rulers"   AD 103–111

SN 37 = *BMC, Imp.* 3, p.84, no.395. *Mint of Rome.*

Obverse: Laureate bust of Trajan; around, IMP. TRAIANO AVG. GER. DAC. P.M. TR.P.

Reverse: River-god reclining and touching the prow of a ship; below, DANVVIVS = the Danube; around, COS.V P.P. S.P.Q.R. OPTIMO PRINC.

The titulature, which runs continuously from obverse to reverse, reflects a dedication by the senate and the Roman people to Trajan in his capacity as *Optimus Princeps* = best of rulers, cf. nos. 91, 93, 97, 99 and 100. The reverse type alludes to the fact that the Danube was now within the Roman Empire after the conquest of the trans-Danubian Dacia. Cf. nos. 85–88.

85   Foundation of Dacica.

SN 479 = *CIL* 3.1443. *Sarmizegetusa (Dacia)*.

On the authority of the emperor Caesar Trajan Augustus, son of deified Nerva, on the occasion of the foundation of the colony of Dacica by the fifth legion *Macedonica*, Scaurianus his propraetorian legate *(set this up)*.

The full title of the colony somewhat later was Ulpia Traiana Augusta Dacica Sarmizegetusa. It retained the name of the old royal capital of Decebalus (see nos. 70 and 86), though it was some distance from it. Its foundation immediately after the conquest may be compared with Claudius' foundation of Camulodunum in Britain only a few years after the invasion. Decimus Terentius Scaurianus was the first governor of Dacia.

86 **(a) Sosius Senecio(?); (b) Licinius Secundus** (a) before AD 114; (b) before 110

SN 219. (a) *Rome, ILS* 1022; (b) *Barcelona (Barcino), Spain, ILS* 1952.

(a) ... the emperor Caesar Nerva Trajan Augustus Germanicus Dacicus conquered in war the Dacian people and king Decebalus. Under the same commander he was propraetorian legate, granted eight silver spearheads, eight silver-mounted banners, two crowns for sieges, two crowns for ramparts[1], two marine crowns, two golden crowns; propraetorian legate of the province of Belgica, legate of the first legion *Minervia*, Caesar's candidate for the praetorship and plebeian tribunate, quaestor of the province of Achaea and member of the four-man commission for the roads. To this man the senate, on the proposal of the emperor Trajan Augustus Germanicus Dacicus decreed triumphal honours, and resolved that a statue be erected at public expense.

(b) For Lucius Licinius Secundus who attended on his patron Lucius Licinius Sura in his first, second and third consulship, member of the six-man college of priests of Augustus of the colony Julia Victrix Triumphalis of Tarraco, and of that of the colony Faventia Julia Augusta Pia of Barcino, by decree of the councillors of Barcino.

(a) C. P. Jones, *JRS* 60 (1970), 98–104, makes it almost certain that the man in question is Sosius Senecio and not (as generally thought hitherto) Licinius Sura. Senecio was consul in 99 and 107 (Dio 68.16.2).

(b) Lucius Licinius Sura came from Spain, like Trajan. The date of his first consulship is unknown; his second was in 102, his third (an exceptional honour) in 107. He may have played some part in the elevation of Trajan in 97, and was one of the most influential men of his time. He may have died in 108. Secundus was Sura's freedman.

87 **Julius Quadratus Bassus**

SN 214 = *Sitzungsber. Akad. Wissensch. München*, 1934. Heft 3. *Pergamum.*

Gaius Julius Quadratus Bassus, consul, *pontifex*, commander in the Dacian war and victorious in that campaign under the emperor Trajan, granted triumphal honours, propraetorian legate of the province of Judaea, propraetorian legate of the province of Cappadocia, Galatia, Lesser Armenia, Pontus, Paphlagonia, Isauria and Pisidia, propraetorian legate of the province of Syria, Phoenicia, Commagene, propraetorian legate of the province of Dacia, military tribune of the thirteenth legion, one of the board of three directors of the Mint, legate of Crete and Cyrene, [curule?] aedile, *praetor peregrinus* of the Roman people, commander of the loyal and faithful eleventh legion *Claudia*, the fourth legion *Scythica*, the ... legion ..., the twelfth legion *Fulminata*, the third legion *Gallica*, the ... legion ..., the thirteenth legion *Gemina* and the ... legion ... He was a man of good birth, descended [from kings or senators?]. To their own founder and patron the city of Seleuceia at the crossing *(set this up)*, through the agency of their delegate ...

[1] See no. 70.

(on the other side)

This man died while still campaigning in Dacia and governing the province. His body was taken to Asia, carried by appointed troops under the command of a senior centurion, Quintilius Capito. A procession for him was led through the whole of the city and military quarters on the express orders of the deified emperor Hadrian. A memorial was provided for him by the fiscus.

The subject of this inscription was consul in 105, and a friend of Trajan. He was probably one of a small group of men of oriental origin, perhaps connected with former royal families, who entered the senate at this time (R. Syme, *Tacitus* 510ff.). His last appointment in Dacia, where he died, was made *c.*117 either by Trajan or Hadrian.

The Seleuceia referred to is Seleuceia on the Euphrates, about 113 kilometres below Samosata. There was an important crossing between it and Apamaea on the opposite bank, and the two together became known as Zeugma = "junction". For other patrons see no. 19 *note*.

88   Altar at Adamklissi.   AD 108–109

SN 303 = *CIL* 3.12467. *Adamklissi (Moesia Inferior).*

To Mars the Avenger the emperor Caesar Nerva Trajan Augustus Germanicus Dacicus, son of deified Nerva, *pontifex maximus*, holder of tribunician power thirteen times, hailed as *Imperator* six times, five times consul, father of his country, [by means of his army?] ... *(dedicated this).*

The monument of Adamklissi in the Dobrudja (Romania) is one of the most substantial in the Balkan provinces. It appears to celebrate both Trajan's conquest of Dacia as well as vengeance (note the dedication to *Mars Ultor*) for heavy Roman losses at the hands of the Dacians in the time of Domitian; cf. no. 70, 85 and 86. It stands beside the Domitianic memorial to the dead.

89   Trajan's public works, *congiaria* and games.   AD 108–113

SN 22. *Consular list (Fasti Ostienses), Ostia.*

108

[The emperor Trajan began to give the third? session] of his second series of gladiatorial shows, which he completed on 30 March in 13 days; 340 pairs of gladiators were involved. 4 June the emperor Trajan began to give his second show. *(gap in text)*
Duovirs: A. Manlius Augustalis, C. Iulius Proculus.

109

A. Cornelius Palma for the second time, P. Calvisius Tullus
1 March   – L. Annius Largus[1]
1 May   – Cn. Antonius Fuscus, C. Iulius Philopappus
1 Sept.   – C. Aburnius Valens, C. Iulius Proculus

[1] Suffect for Palma.

22 June the emperor Nerva Trajan Caesar Augustus Germanicus Dacicus dedicated his baths and opened them to the public. 24 June he dedicated the water-supply,[1] named after himself, that ran through the whole of the city. 1 Nov. the emperor Trajan completed his gift in 117 days with 4,941½ pairs of gladiators. 11 Nov. the emperor Trajan dedicated his site for sea battles in which for 6 days 127½ pairs of gladiators fought, and finished it 24 Nov..
Duovirs: M. Valerius Euphemianus, C. Valerius Iustus.

110

M. Peducaeus Priscinus, Ser. Scipio Orfitus
C. Avidius Nigrinus, Ti. Iulius Aquila
L. Catilius Severus, C. Erucianus Silo
A. Larcius Priscus, Sex. Marius Honoratus
Duovirs: P. Naevius Severus, D. Nonius Pompilianus

111

C. Calpurnius Piso, M. Vettius Bolanus
1 May – T. Avidius Quietus, L. Eggius Marullus
        L. Octavius Crassus, P. Coelius Apollinaris
Duovirs with censorial powers for 5 years: C. Nasennius Marcellus, for the third time, patron of the colony, C. Valerius Iustus.

112

The emperor Nerva Trajan Caesar Augustus Germanicus Dacicus, for the sixth time,
T. Sextius Africanus.
[13 Jan. ?M.?] Licinius Ruso[2]
Cn. Cornelius Severus, Q. Valerius Vegetus
P. Stertinius Quartus, T. Julius Maximus
C. Claudius Severus, T. Settidius Firmus
1 Jan. the emperor Trajan dedicated his Forum and the Basilica Ulpia.
30 Jan. the emperor Trajan gave games in three theatres for fifteen days; during them presents were thrown on three days, and 1 March circus games were given, thirty rounds, on which day he gave a feast for the senate and the equestrian class. 25 June the emperor Trajan now began to give ... 29 Aug. Marciana Augusta[3] died and was named *diva (i.e. deified)*. On the same day Matidia[4] was named Augusta. 3 Sept. Marciana Augusta was buried with a state funeral. The emperor Trajan began to give the rest of the shows equal to the previous ones and the day was named that of the vintage. 22 Aug. the temple of Vulcan that had fallen into ruin from age, but had been restored with additional decoration, was dedicated.
Duovirs: Longus Grattianus Caninianus, Fadius Probianus.

---

[1] Cf. SN 382 = *ILS* 290.
[2] Suffect for Trajan.
[3] Trajan's sister, cf. SN 134 = *BMC, Imp.* 3, p.126, no.653.
[4] Daughter of Marciana, cf. SN 108 = *BMC, Imp.* 3, p.108, no.531.

113

L. Publilius Celsus, for the second time, C. Clodius Crispinus.
Ser. Cornelius Dolabella.[1]

L. Stertinius Noricus, L. Fadius Rufinus.
Cn. Cornelius Urbicus, T. Sempronius Rufinus.
... May the third set of gifts was made together with games involving 1,202
pairs of gladiators. 12 May the emperor Trajan dedicated the temple of
Venus in Caesar's Forum and the column in his own Forum.[2] 14 May ...

The great public works, *congiaria* ("distributions") and games between 108
and 113 owed their financial backing to the fruits of the Dacian Wars. From
these too came the prisoners for the shows. The Trajanic Forum was the largest
of the imperial *fora*, occupying, with its associated buildings, an area five times
that of the Forum of Augustus. The architect was Apollodorus, builder of
Trajan's Danubian bridge. For the lavishness of Trajan's games, see also Dio
68.15.

90   Trajan's column.   AD 112–113

SN 378a = *ILS* 294. *Base of Trajan's column, Rome.*

The senate and people of Rome *(put this up)* for the emperor Caesar Nerva
Trajan Augustus Germanicus Dacicus, son of deified Nerva, *pontifex
maximus*, holder of tribunician power seventeen times, hailed as *Imperator*
six times, consul six times, father of his country, to show how high was
the hill and place that was removed by such great public works.

The area referred to is that of the forum and markets of Trajan. The markets
are built up the sides of a slope, which seems to have been completely cut away,
and provide large numbers of shops reached by stairs and covered ways. The
column itself bears in a continuous spiral carved on it the whole story of the
Dacian wars. This is not only an original masterpiece but an important, if sometimes confusing, source of information about the course of the war and the
Roman army of the period. See next item, and J. Carcopino, *Daily Life in Ancient
Rome*, 15ff.

91   Denarius of Trajan: Trajan's column.   AD 112–114

SN 378b = *BMC, Imp.* 3, p.94, no.454. *Mint of Rome.*

Obverse: Laureate bust of Trajan; around, IMP. TRAIANO AVG. GER.
DAC. P.M. TR.P. COS.VI P.P.

Reverse: Trajan's column; around, S.P.Q.R. OPTIMO PRINCIPI = the
senate and Roman people to the best of rulers.

Trajan was regularly described as *Optimus* ("best") from *c*.112, cf. nos. 84,
93, 97, 99, 100, and previous item, but it does not seem to have become offi-
cially part of his name until 114.

---

[1] Suffect for Celsus.
[2] Cf. nos. 90–91.

92 Sestertius of Trajan: improvement of the harbour at the mouth of the Tiber.
AD 112–114

SN 385 = *BMC, Imp.* 3, p.205*. *Mint of Rome.*

Obverse: Laureate bust of Trajan; around, IMP. CAES. NERVAE TRAIANO AVG. GER. DAC. P.M. TR.P.COS.VI P.P.

Reverse: Harbour surrounded by buildings and containing three ships; below, S C; around, PORTVM TRAIANI = the harbour of Trajan.

Trajan undertook a considerable extension and improvement of Claudius' work on the harbour on the opposite side of the Tiber from Ostia.

93 The Via Traiana.   (a) AD 108–109; (b) 113–114; (c) 112–114

SN 408. (a) *on the Via Traiana between Beneventum and Aequum Tuticum (ILS 5866);*
      (b) *on the arch at Beneventum (ILS 296);*
      (c) *aureus, Mint of Rome. (BMC, Imp.* 3, p.98, no.484).

(a) The emperor Caesar Nerva Trajan Augustus Germanicus Dacicus, son of deified Nerva, *pontifex maximus,* holder of tribunician power thirteen times, hailed as *Imperator* six times, consul five times, father of his country, built the road and bridges from Beneventum to Brundisium at his own expense.

(b) The senate and people of Rome *(put this up)* for the emperor Caesar Nerva Trajan Optimus Augustus Germanicus Dacicus, son of deified Nerva, *pontifex maximus,* holder of tribunician power eighteen times, hailed as *Imperator* seven times, consul six times, father of his country, mightiest ruler.

(c) *Obverse:* Laureate bust of Trajan; around, IMP. TRAIANO AVG. GER. DAC. P.M. TR.P. COS.VI P.P.

Reverse: Reclining woman holding wheel; below, VIA TRAIANA; around, S.P.Q.R. OPTIMO PRINCIPI = the senate and people of Rome to the best of rulers.

In spite of the fact that Trajan was from outside Italy, more rather than less attention appears to have been paid by him to the state of Italy, with new improved harbours (see previous item), roads, and above all the *alimenta* scheme (see nos. 80–81).

94 Road-building in Arabia Nabataea.   AD 110–111

SN 420 = *ILS* 5834. *Milestone near Thoana, 54 Roman miles (approx. 80 km.) north of Petra.*

The emperor Caesar Nerva Trajan Augustus Germanicus Dacicus, son of deified Nerva, *pontifex maximus,* holder of tribunician power fifteen times, hailed as *Imperator* six times, consul five times, father of his country, when Arabia had been turned into a province, opened up and paved a new road from the borders of Syria to the Red Sea through the agency of Gaius Claudius Severus, imperial propraetorian legate. LIIII.

Arabia Nabataea had long been client, and was provincialised between 105 and 108. The road referred to in the inscription ran from Damascus to the Gulf of Akaba and was of great importance to the traders between the Roman empire and India.

95   Early career of Hadrian.   AD 112

SN 109 = *ILS* 308. *Theatre of Dionysus, Athens.*

For Publius Aelius Hadrian, son of Publius, of the tribe *Sergia*, consul,[1] member of the board of seven for supervising sacrificial banquets, priest of Augustus, propraetorian legate of the emperor Nerva Trajan Caesar Augustus Germanicus Dacicus in Lower Pannonia,[2] praetor and at the same time legate of the loyal and faithful first legion *Minervia* in the Dacian campaign,[3] plebeian tribune,[4] quaestor of the emperor Trajan and on his staff in the Dacian campaign,[5] twice granted military awards by Trajan, tribune of the loyal and faithful second legion *Adiutrix*, of the fifth legion *Macedonica*, of the loyal and faithful twenty-second legion *Primigenia*,[6] *sevir* of a squadron of Roman knights, prefect of the Latin festival, *decemvir* of the board of lawsuits.

The council of the Areopagus and that of the six hundred and the Assembly of Athens made Hadrian their Archon.[7]

This inscription gives us Hadrian's career up to 112. Consul at the age of 32, his career marked him out as the obvious potential successor. His future phil-hellenic policy is foreshadowed by the honour of being Archon of Athens, the only private Roman citizen ever to hold the position.

96   Career and Will of Pliny the Younger.   Before AD 114

SN 230 = *ILS* 2927. *Milan (probably originally from Comum).*

Gaius Plinius Caecilius Secundus, son of Lucius, of the tribe *Oufentina*, consul,[8] augur, propraetorian legate[9] of the province of Pontus and Bithynia, sent to that province with consular power in accordance with a decree of the senate by the emperor Caesar Nerva Trajan Augustus Germanicus Dacicus, father of his country; curator[10] of the Tiber bed and river-banks and of the sewers of the city; prefect of the treasury of Saturn[11]; prefect of the *aerarium militare*[12]; praetor[13]; plebeian tribune[14]; imperial

---

[1] Suffect 108.
[2] 107.
[3] 106, the second Dacian War.
[4] 105.
[5] 101–102, the first Dacian War.
[6] 95,96,97 respectively.
[7] The first paragraph is in Latin, the second in Greek.
[8] 100. He delivered in honour of Trajan a *gratiarum actio*, known in its published form as the Panegyricus.
[9] 111 onwards.
[10] 104–105.
[11] 98–100.
[12] Between 94 and 97.
[13] 93.
[14] 92.

quaestor[1]; *sevir* of Roman knights; military tribune of the third legion *Gallica*[2]; *Decemvir* of the board of lawsuits. He left ... sesterces in his will for the construction of baths with an additional sum of 300,000 sesterces *(more?)* for their decoration and a further 200,000 for their upkeep. For the support of his own freedmen, 100 in number, he likewise bequeathed to the town 1,866,666 sesterces, the income from which he wished afterwards to be used for an annual banquet for the townspeople. In his lifetime he also gave 500,000 sesterces for the support of boys and girls of families living in the city, and also a library and 100,000 sesterces for the upkeep of the library.

This inscription recording the younger Pliny's career and bequests to his home town was placed on the baths built in Como as a result of Pliny's bequest.

For imperial *alimenta* schemes see nos. 80 and 81. Pliny describes the setting up of his bequest in *Letters* 7. 18.2; cf. 1.8.10. 1.8 refers to the official opening of the library in 97.

97 Mancian tenures in Africa. AD 116–117

SN 463 = *FIRA* 1.100. *Henchir-Mettich, north of Thignica (Africa).*

For the safety of our Augustus, the emperor Caesar Trajan, *princeps*, and of the whole divine house of Optimus Germanicus Parthicus.

Laid down by Licinius Maximus and by Felicior, freedman of the emperor, procurators of Augustus, following the example of the Mancian law.

Those of them who *(shall dwell?)* within the estate of the country house Magna Variana, also known as Mappalia Siga, are permitted under the Mancian law to cultivate those fields which are left over so that the cultivator has the use of them as his own. From the crops arising in that place they will have to present shares under the Mancian law to the owners, tenants-in-chief or managers of the estate on the following conditions:

The smallholders are to render to the tenants-in-chief or managers of the estate on their own reckoning the totals of the growth of each crop which they will have to carry to the threshing floor and process; and if the tenants-in-chief or managers of the estate in return send notice of precisely what shares will be due from the smallholders, the smallholders shall in good faith[3] guarantee in writing the shares of that corn which they must deliver, and they must present the said shares to the tenants-in-chief or managers of the estate.

Those who have country houses on the estate of Magna Variana or Mappalia Siga, will keep them and will have to present to the owners of the estate or to the tenants-in-chief or managers the owners' share of crops and grapes or whatever is the usual fashion of the Mancian law: (required portions are as follows):

wheat from the threshing floor – a third;
barley from the threshing floor – a third;

---

[1] Under Domitian, cf. *Letters.* 7.16.2.
[2] In Syria.
[3] Or "with impunity".

beans – a quarter (or a fifth?);
wine from the vat – a third;
processed oil – a third;
honey from beehives – one *sextarius* from each hive.

If anyone has more than five hives at the time of gathering the honey on each occasion, then he will have to give ... to the owners, tenants-in-chief or managers of the estate. If anyone transfers hives, swarms, bees or jars of honey from the estate of Magna Variana or Mappalia Siga onto land subject to the eight-each rule for the purpose of defrauding the owners, tenants-in-chief or managers of the estate, then all hives, swarms, bees and honey-jars on the estate will be forfeited to the owners, tenants-in-chief or managers of the estate.

Dried figs from trees outside the orchard, where the orchard is within the estate itself so that ... no more, the smallholder will have to give a ... part on his own reckoning of the collected fruit to the tenant-in-chief or manager of the estate. Old plantations of figs or olives which were sown before this law must, as is usual, have their crop presented to the tenant-in-chief or manager of the estate. But if any fig plantation is created later, the crop of that plantation over a period of five successive gatherings, on his own reckoning, is allowed to the sower: after the fifth gathering by the same aforementioned law the crop will have to be presented to the tenants-in-chief or managers of the estate.

It is permitted to sow and cultivate vines in place of old ones on condition that during the first five harvestings from the *(time of)* sowing the sower on his own reckoning may receive the harvest of such vines, and likewise after the fifth harvest from such a sowing a whole third of the harvest will have to be given by the Mancian law to the tenants-in-chief or managers of that *(estate)*. Sowing and cultivating an olive plantation where idle land will be brought under cultivation should also be permitted on condition that for the first ten crops, on his own reckoning, from the sowing of such an olive plantation be allowed *(to the sower)* and likewise after ten crops a third of the oil produced will have to be given to the tenants-in-chief or managers of the estate. The grafter of wild olives after five years will have to give a third.

The *(fields?)* on the estate of Magna Variana or Mappalia Siga, except those fields which have vetch, must have their crops given to the tenants-in-chief or managers; the guards will have to exact them. In the case of the flocks which graze within the estate of Magna Variana or Mappalia Siga, for each head a fixed sum of four *asses* will have to be presented to the tenants-in-chief or managers of the owners of the estate. If anyone on the estate of Magna Variana or Mappalia Siga cuts, decapitates, removes, transfers, burns, desecrates (?) any crops which are standing, hanging, ripe or unripe, the loss *(will have to be made up)* to the tenants-in-chief or managers of the estate *(by the smallholder?)* whose duty it will be to present so much ...

A man who has or will have improved the surface of uncultivated land or who has or will have erected a building, or who after improvements has

or will have ceased the same; from the time the said surface ceased or will
cease to be worked such improvements will be preserved in accordance
with the rights of cultivation in force at the time or whenever provided
that the improvements have been kept during the first period of two years
after cessation of work: after the two-year period their tenants-in-chief or
managers ... A surface which was cultivated the previous year and has
ceased to be cultivated should be the subject of a declaration by the tenant-
in-chief or manager of the estate against the man said to own the surface
... it is declared by declaration ... by calling witnesses and likewise he ...
for the following year and without complaint from him after a period of
two years the tenant-in-chief or manager is to *(order him to?)* cultivate ...

Tenants living on the estate of Magna *(Variana)* or Mappalia Siga [must
each carry out] each year for the owners, tenants-in-chief [or managers]
two days' labour in [ploughing?] and two days' labour at harvest-time.
Cottage-tenants? of the estate within ... of a year ... their names to the
tenants-in-chief [or managers] ... as guards ... Those living [on the estate
of Magna *(Variana)* or] Mappalia Siga who pay *stipendium* ... for the
tenants-in-chief or managers ... guards of the estate ... imperial slaves.

(At the foot of col. (i)) This law was inscribed by Lurius Victor [?son
of] Odilo in charge, Flavius Geminius mason, and Felix [?son of] Annobal
Birzil ...

The emperor was the largest landowner in the Empire, and his estates were
run by procurators who leased to *coloni*, who paid, in Africa, a certain number
of days' work and a share of the crops. Sometimes land was first leased to a
tenant-in-chief *(conductor)* who sublet. Shortage of labour in the first and
second centuries led to special terms to attract people to take up unused land.
The Mancian law offered both a sort of semi-ownership on such land when
cultivated (sale only excluded) and rent-free occupation for five to ten years
according to the crops grown. It is not known who was the originator of the
Mancian law; a proconsul of Flavian date is a possibility. Mancian tenures still
survived in Africa in the sixth century.

98   Jewish revolt in Cyrene.   AD 118–119

SN 59 = *SEG* 9.252. *Milestone 5 Roman miles (= 7.4 km.) from Cyrene on the
road to Apollonia.*

The emperor Caesar Trajan Hadrian Augustus, son of deified Trajan
Parthicus and grandson of deified Nerva, *pontifex maximus*, holder of
tribunician power twice, consul three times, restored through [?the soldiers
of the cohort ...] the road which had been blocked and severely damaged
during the Jewish revolt.

Cyrene and its roads received severe damage in the Jewish revolt which broke
out in 115. The Apollonia road would be damaged because thereby communi-
cations between Cyrene and its port would be cut. R. G. Goodchild, *Papers of
the British School at Rome*, 18 (1950), 86, records a similarly worded Hadrianic
milestone beside the North Gate of Cyrene on the road to Apollonia. Both mile-
stones indicate that the Hadrianic restoration of Cyrene included repair of

road-damage. Cf. SN 424 (= *SEG* 9.251; 13.619*b*) for a Trajanic milestone on
the same road.

99   Sestertius of Trajan: Armenia and Mesopotamia reduced.   AD 116–117

SN 50 = *BMC, Imp.* 3, p.221, no.1035. *Mint of Rome.*

> *Obverse:* Laureate bust of Trajan; around, IMP.CAES.NER.TRAIANO
> OPTIMO AVG. GER. DAC. PARTHICO P.M. TR.P. COS.VI P.P.

> *Reverse:* Trajan standing with Armenia at his feet; on either side, S C;
> around, ARMENIA ET MESOPOTAMIA IN POTESTATEM P.R.
> REDACTAE = Armenia and Mesopotamia *(have been brought)* under
> the sway of the Roman people.

100 Deified Trajan.   After August AD 117

SN 105 = *ILS* 304. *Aratispi (Baetica), Spain.*

> To the emperor Caesar deified Trajan Optimus Germanicus Dacicus
> Parthicus, son of deified Nerva, *pontifex maximus*, holder of tribunician
> power twenty-one times, hailed as *Imperator* thirteen times, consul six
> times, father of his country, the best and greatest *princeps*, saviour of the
> human race, the community of Aratispi decreed this, dedicating it after he
> had been deified.

Trajan died early August 117, and was accorded divine honours.

CONCORDANCES

A.

EJ	L.8						
39	9		100	35		298	62
49	10		144	40		347	82
51	15		145	41		372	70
53	13		160	45		408	63
69	1		228	42		453 (parts)	67
85	16		231(c)	30		454 (parts)	68
87	2		259	37		531	48
90	11		262	36			
94a	8		268	38		SN	L.8
97	18		365	31		15	73
101	4		368	33		22	89
102	3		369	34		27(a)	74
134	5		370	27		27(b)	75
163	20		391	50		29	77
182	6		392	51		30	78
217	14		407	32		37	84
218a	17					50	99
220	12		MW	L.8		59	98
225	21		1	55		91	76
243	22		14 (lines 62–65)	69		105	100
245	23		31	49		109	95
320	7		38	52		214	87
333	24		40	54		219	86
345	25		51	56		230	96
354	19		53	65		303	88
			58	71		314	79
			64	72		378(a)	90
SG	L.8		66	74		378(b)	91
32	26		105	64		385	92
43(a)	28		108	66		408	93
43(b)	29		151	57		420	94
51(b)	43		237	60		435 (parts)	80
53	44		239	59		437	81
57	39		244	61		463	97
64	46		271	58		479	85
70	47		274	53		493(a)	83

B.

AHMJ	L.8						
8	55		40	22		140	51
23	34		43	24		141	33
27	42		87	94		166	3
30	96		93	68			
32	95		94	67		*AJP*	L.8
			96	27		(1954) p.225	8

Arch. Anz.	*L.8*	5. 4922	19	pp.394–7	32(b)
(1940), 521	21	5. 5050	33	(1924)	
		5. 5262	96	pp.77–8	32(a)
BMC, Imp. 1	*L.8*	6. 385	9		
p.129, nos. 70ff	10	6. 472	74	*FIRA*	*L.8*
p.130, nos. 76ff	2	6. 798	82	1. 15	55
p.162, no.104	6	6. 920	29	1. 23 (parts)	67
p.168, no.29	28	6. 921	35	1. 24 (parts)	68
p.214, note*	44	6. 930	55	1. 43	34
p.250, no.257	40	6. 934	57	1. 45	31
p.251, no.261	39	6. 944	65	1. 58	50
p.294, note*	47(c)	6. 945	66	1. 59	51
p.295, no.19	47(d)	6. 960	90	1. 70	32(b)
p.297, no.31	47(a)	6. 1257	63(a)	1. 71	33
p.299, no.38	47(b)	6. 1258	63(b)	1.100	97
p.306, no.65	52	6. 1402	54	3.117 (parts)	80
		6. 1444	86(a)		
*BMC, Imp.*3	*L.8*	6. 1492	81	Gordon	*L.8*
p.1, no.4	76(a)	6. 2065		103	35
p.3, no.16	75	(lines 62–65)	69	109	30
p.4, no.22	76(b)	6.10213	13	135	56
p.8, no.59	76(d)	6.32367		148 (parts)	69
p.9, no.63	76(e)	(lines 62–65)	69	153	72
p.10, no.68	76(f)	8. 13	49		
p.21, no.115	77	8. 1026	71	*IG*	*L.8*
p.21, no.118	76(c)	8. 7058	62	2/3².3278	41
p.21, no.119	78	8.25902	97	7.2713	46
p.84, no.395	84	9. 1455 (parts)	80	14.2012	72
p.94, no.454	91	9. 1558	93(b)		
p.98, no.484	93(c)	9. 6005	93(a)	*IGRR*	*L.8*
p.205, *	92	10. 1401	31	1. 350–2	72
p.221, no.1035	99	10. 3853	58	1.1263	50
		10. 4862	23	3. 133	60
CIL	*L.8*	10.6225	53	4.1086	36
2. 172	26	10.7852	51		
2. 1963 (parts)	67	11. 1421	1	*ILA*	*L.8*
2. 1964 (parts)	68	11. 3303	4	2.644	62
2. 2054	100	11. 3805	24		
2. 4536	86(b)	11. 3872	16	*ILGN*	*L.8*
3. 318	64	11. 4170	15	633	14
3. 550	95	11. 7283	12		
3. 1443	85	12. 1849	18	*ILS*	*L.8*
3. 6741	43	12. 5842	37	95	9
3.12467	88	13. 1668	34	140	1
3.14149²¹⁻²²	94	14. 3608	42	154	4
3.14195⁴	83			157	15
3.14387a	59	*CRAI*	*L.8*	159	16
5. 1838	22	(1915)		189	18

190	26	8794	46	1933.241	56	
206	33	8795	60	1947. 49	8	
212	34	8958	59			
214	78 (ref. only)	8996	12	*Nouvelles archives*		
216	29	9200	70	*des missions*	*L.8*	
218	63	9235	45	1913.38	25	
222	35					
232	43	*IRT*	*L.8*	*OGIS*	*L.8*	
244	55	330	17	379	60	
252	57	537	49	583	5	
263	64			669	50	
264	65	**LR**	*L.8*			
265	66	16	1	*P.Lond.*	*L.8*	
274	74	21	55	1912	27	
294	90	22	65			
296	93(b)	27	29	*RIB*	*L.8*	
304	100	28	42	12	38	
308	95	31	82	330	79	
983	54	32	33–34	(*see also* LACTOR		
985	53	39	94	4)		
986	42	42	97			
992	58	50	31	*SEG*	*L.8*	
1022	86(a)	83	67–68	9.252	98	
1321	37	89	80	11.922–3	3	
1349	22	90	96	16.861	50	
1448	82	96	27			
1952	86(b)	98	50	*Sel.Pap.*	*L.8*	
2127	71	104	46	211	7	
2690	23	106, 168	7	212	27	
2927	96	167	69			
5177	72	168	8	*SIG³*	*L.8*	
5834	94			804	36	
5866	93(a)	*Mélanges de*		814	46	
5947	51	*l'Univ. St.*				
6043	31	*Jos.Beyrouth*	*L.8*	*Sitzungsber.Akad.*		
6044	13	25 (1942–3)		*Wissensch.*		
6088 (parts)	67	p.32	61	*München*	*L.8*	
6089 (parts)	68			1934, Heft 3	87	
6099	19	*Mélanges*				
6106	81	*Gautier*	*L.8*	*YCS*	*L.8*	
6509 (parts)	80	(1937) p.332	20	7 (1940)	73	
6579	24				(ref. only)	
7193	83	*NdS*	*L.8*			
		1924.514	11			

INDICES
The numbers refer to entries, not pages.

(a) ARMY UNITS

(b) GODS AND GODDESSES

(c) TITLES

(d) NAMES OF PERSONS

Emperors in capitals. Names occurring only incidentally are on the whole omitted.

(e) NAMES OF PLACES AND TRIBES
(the latter in capitals)

Printed in the United States
by Baker & Taylor Publisher Services.

Printed in the United States
by Baker & Taylor Publisher Services